Praise for

THE PERFECTION DETOX

"In *The Perfection Detox,* Petra Kolber teaches us recovering people-pleasers beset by anxiety and impossible standards how to embrace our cracks to find our light. I can't think of a more joyful, authentic, perfectly imperfect person to be the messenger for this movement. It's time to transform our inner prisons into freedom and joy by celebrating the very flaws that make us who we are."

—JENNY BLAKE, author of
Pivot: The Only Move That Matters Is Your Next One

"Petra is a guiding light to all of us who don't feel like we are enough. Perfectionism is an unnecessary epidemic and this book could not be more relevant or timely. If you give yourself a hard time and want to feel like the worthy, confident, whole person that you truly are at your core, this is a must read."

—SUSIE MOORE, confidence coach and author of
What If It Does Work Out?

"Petra's understanding and personal recovery from perfectionism is not just a fresh concept worth reading about, it is a deeply lived success story that absolutely everyone can resonate with to one degree or another. Follow the practices outlined in this book and watch your life, health, happiness, and ability to take control of your world shift beyond measure. This is required reading for anyone who has ever said the words; 'must,' 'should,' 'have to' or, 'When everything is perfect . . . then I'll try!'"

—MELANIE SMITH, executive coach, heartbreak specialist,
brand expert, entrepreneur, writer, actor, yogi, and mother

"Thank you for this book! Not only for 'perfectionists' but a gentle, powerful, and effective handbook for anyone on the quest for inner peace, higher consciousness, and a beautiful abundant life."

—MISTY TRIPOLI, creator of The GROOVE Method® and
founder of The World GROOVE Movement™

"This heartfelt offering from a reformed perfectionist is an ideal way to meet your fear, anxiety, and self-deprecation head-on with insightful narrative and activity. It will put you on your journey to guided inquiry, facilitating the transformation to a less 'perfect' you. Thank you, Petra Kolber, for creating this contemplative tool to support the quest to become the happiest version of ourselves."

—TAMI REILLY, associate athletic director for fitness and wellness
at Quinnipiac University, and international fitness presenter

THE
PERFECTION
DETOX

THE
PERFECTION
DETOX

Tame Your Inner Critic, Live Bravely,
and Unleash Your Joy

Petra Kolber

Da Capo
LIFE
LONG

Da Capo Press
Hachette Book Group
1290 Avenue of the Americas, New York, NY 10104
www.dacapopress.com
@DaCapoPress

Printed in the United States of America
First Edition: August 2018
Published by Da Capo Press, an imprint of Perseus Books, LLC, a subsidiary of Hachette Book Group, Inc. The Da Capo Press name and logo is a trademark of the Hachette Book Group.

The Hachette Speakers Bureau provides a wide range of authors for speaking events. To find out more, go to www.hachettespeakersbureau.com or call (866) 376-6591. The publisher is not responsible for websites (or their content) that are not owned by the publisher.

Print book interior design by Linda Mark.

Library of Congress Cataloging-in-Publication Data has been applied for.

ISBNs: 978-0-7382-3485-4 (trade paperback), 978-0-7382-3484-7 (ebook)
LSC-C
10 9 8 7 6 5 4 3 2 1

For my perfect sister, Jennie

*and in memory of our mother, Gwenda, who never
expected us to be perfect, she only wanted us to be happy.*

Instructions for living a life. Pay attention. Be astonished. Tell about it.

—MARY OLIVER

Contents

THE
PERFECTION
DETOX

Introduction

SO HOW DOES A RECOVERING PERFECTIONIST WRITE THE PERFECT INTRODUCTION? HOW does she craft an opening paragraph in which she earns your trust, and where you will fall in love with every one of those words? How does she write an opening built upon the wish that you will be seized suddenly by the feeling that you are about to have an encounter with a trusted friend?

The answer is, she doesn't. She doesn't, I don't, no one does . . . no one knows how to write that perfect page. And this represents the quintessential perfectionist's predicament: what we are striving for, and what actually exists, can never meet.

So the question then becomes, do I stop because it is impossible, or do I start because I believe this book will make a difference in your life?

Because I have done the work to rewire my perfectionist's mindset, I was able to begin. I have created and crafted something and released it out into the world, flaws and all.

So, as I began doing the thing that terrified me, that is, writing this first page, I realized that this was the perfect metaphor for how perfection can shape and distort our lives. If I had waited for the perfect word, the perfect introduction, or the perfect moment to begin, this book would never have been written.

While it is impossible for us to get to know each other in a couple of paragraphs, perfect or not, what I hope you can sense is that you and I are kindred warrior sisters. I get you, I understand you, and we have gone through many of the same internal battles.

One of the reasons that I decided to write *The Perfection Detox* is that I know how lonely the planet of perfection is. I hope that as you finish reading this book, you will feel more of an insider than an outsider, more connected to the women you see all around you, and more empowered to start living your life—a life that is rooted in joy and lived on your terms.

I also consider it an immense privilege to be alongside you for this journey. While our backstories are different, I understand the deep pain and the constant struggle that come from living a life constantly monitored and judged by perfection.

There is a different way of moving through your days. A way of living that allows you to dance with your dreams instead of dodging potential mistakes. A life rooted in optimism, joy, potential, and possibility. A life that is waiting for you to take a spin with her, fully engaged with your heart and soul.

Now is the moment to take the first step back to your authentic self and toward your abundant future, as you would not have picked up this book (unless you thought this was a book on juicing) if you believed perfection was working in your favor. Before we get to those steps, it's important first to think about what we mean when we expect perfection; what is this "perfect" that we're so infatuated with?

FIRST THINGS FIRST: DEFINING PERFECTIONISM

To say that something is a perfect fit is to suggest that there could be nothing better. To do something perfectly means to have completed a task with a sort of divine level of skill and to have produced a product that is spotless, flawless, pristine. Culturally, we have been taught that perfectionism is something to be proud of.

But true perfectionists are unlikely to ever experience feelings of pride or satisfaction. They are more likely to feel disappointment and despair, perpetually dogged by the belief that they or others haven't reached the golden ring of a flawless and faultless life. And therein lies the tortuous problem: perfect doesn't exist; it's nothing more than a subjective, slippery conjuring of one's mind. Perfectionism, while not a disease of the body, is a cancer of the spirit and one that if left unmanaged will cause great damage to our life.

"Perfect" is only a word until you attach a feeling or expectation to it. Some people might be ambitious, have high standards, and strive to be virtuous without being a perfectionist. Perfectionism, as a personality feature, does not guarantee success; moreover, there is overwhelming evidence to suggest that perfectionism is, ironically, an obstacle to achievement of potential.

The key to reaching the highest level of success is a certain willingness to take risks, which perfectionists viscerally try to avoid for fear of making a mistake. Part of the journey of becoming better, whether as a person or in a skill, is having the fortitude and the wisdom to manage and learn with mistakes, stumbling blocks, and disappointment. A nonperfectionist will see a mishap as a mini milestone on the road to success, or check it off as a character-building experience to be folded into the fabric of growth. But a perfectionist sees a mistake as an affront, an intruder to wrestle to the ground. It is not surprising, therefore, that while the perfectionist plays it safe by retreating, the ambitious nonperfectionist soars.

Of course, this won't be a part of every perfectionist's experience. Perfectionism is not an affliction that replicates itself in every person. It can affect different parts of your life and isn't always self-directed. While it's most common for perfectionism to influence the relationship you have with yourself, it can also manifest in your relationships with other people, including family members, and the relationship you have with work. It takes some exploration of our own lives to determine where perfection is most prevalent, and this is an exploration I'll help guide you through in this book.

Part of this detox will include assessing the role of expectations and standards in your life, and identifying the difference between being ambitious and striving for perfection (hint: one comes with pain and suffering, the other does not). Being able to spot the difference requires asking yourself some difficult questions. Or rather, asking some questions that might at first seem difficult to answer, if only because we don't often study ourselves, except perhaps to criticize, but rarely to just observe and take notes.

Some of the questions and topics you'll need to ponder include: Are the standards you set for yourself reasonable or so unrealistically high that your inner critic is impossible to turn off? Do you see failures as lessons along the way or as catastrophic setbacks, no matter how insignificant? Do you ever allow yourself to celebrate your success or do you immediately place your gaze on the next milestone ahead?

These are the types of explorations that will help you uncover which beliefs and behaviors are working in your favor and which are stopping you from enjoying the life that you are working so hard to create. In *The Perfection Detox,* we'll practice enriching the former, and expelling the latter.

Without a doubt, there are going to be aspects of your awesome personality that you may not necessarily want to discard. Your ability to get projects across the finish line in a timely manner, your organizational skills, your reliability in relationships, and your willingness to go the extra mile in whatever you are doing are all wonderful attributes that may have become entangled with your perfectionistic roots. This is why we will work carefully and with compassion with the intention of making sure that you deliver your best, while also feeling your best at the same time.

One thing I know for sure is that one of the most painful experiences to come out of perfectionism is the feeling of isolation, and in this place of separation it is impossible to flourish and thrive. We tend to feel that we are entirely alone in this suffering; that we are the only ones to experience anxiety and depression as the result of a mistake or falling short of a goal, or to feel that we are being crushed by all of the standards expected of us today. I am here to tell you that we perfectionists are more alike in these struggles than we are different.

WHEN PERFECT WENT VIRAL

This is a prolific time for perfectionism, mostly thanks to social media. The filters, endless takes, and frozen moments featured across a growing list of platforms can make it seem as if everyone else is living a perfect life. Everyone but you, that is. For perfectionists, this perception can spark an obsession with the need to keep up with or surpass the lives of others, or to compare to the point of feeling crippled. Among the thousands of women I have talked to and worked with, I would estimate that over 90 percent of them have shared that they silently struggle to try and not compare themselves to the images of perfection that cross their screens. While even nonperfectionists will casually flirt with comparison, they aren't nearly as susceptible to falling into a destructive relationship with it as us perfectionists. In most cases, this susceptibility is such an ingrained part of who we are that we are not even aware of it, likely because its origins occurred so long ago.

The seeds of perfectionism are often planted early in life, by way of genetic origins or childhood experiences. As my own story will reveal, children of alcoholics are especially prone to becoming perfectionists. Perfectionism gets activated as a vehicle to try to protect our environment and maintain the illusion that our family is just the same as everyone else's, and we also desperately desire to create some semblance of control. We see perfection as a tool to fit in, never make a ripple, and pretend that we have mastery over our life.

But in practice, instead of the picket-fence, prize-winning life, perfectionism leaves us with a bounty of psychological distress. To perpetually strive for unattainable perfection means to fear failure, to avoid risk, to swim in doubt and anxiety, and to normalize negativity. Nothing is ever good enough for the perfectionist, and the world around us reinforces the illusion.

The body, in many cases, can become an object of hyper-focus for perfectionists, especially for women. We are more prone to placing extreme emphasis on self-presentation, which can influence eating behaviors and lay the groundwork for eating disorders to develop.

While not everyone's perfectionism will take them this far, many women fall into the trap of viewing the latest diet or weight-loss fad as a bright and shining beacon, the path to happiness that has thus far eluded them. As women, we have become convinced that as our waistlines shrink, the success and love we experience will expand. We keep setting goals that are either impossible to fulfill or come at a price too high.

When I was younger, I had both anorexia and bulimia, two disorders that kept me separated from being able to live in the present moment and step into my full potential. Never able to be thin enough to satisfy my need for control or eat enough to satisfy my loneliness, I lost six of my best years to a dysfunctional relationship with food. The false illusion of mastery kept me isolated, ridden with anxiety and wrapped in shame.

Many of the women I've spoken to over the years, while not always having dealt with an eating disorder, share the mounting pressure they feel as they try to keep up with the photographs and videos they see every day. We have become so used to the airbrushed and Photoshopped version of reality that we no longer know the difference between realistic and impossible-to-meet expectations. It's absolute madness, and the message it sends has many worried about how to raise daughters with a strong sense of self-esteem or how to protect them from the dangers of trying to live up to what is on their news feed.

If you have young daughters or nieces, I hope this book will give you strategies to help them be the best version of themselves (instead of perhaps trying to replicate their favorite Instagram or reality star). I also hope that in the pages ahead, you will discover how to release the anchor of unrealistic expectations before it sinks you. For me, these expectations multiplied exponentially, until I found myself in desperate need of a detox.

MY PATH TO THE PERFECTION DETOX

There was a time in my life when I thought I had it all figured out. Professionally I was climbing the ranks just about as fast as anyone could in the mid-nineties. By trading in my dance shoes for fitness sneakers, my background in musical theater became a catalyst for my fast-found success as a popular aerobics instructor in New York City. I became a sought-after fitness expert, starring in many best-selling DVDs, working with a range of celebrities from Olympians Nancy Kerrigan and Dara Torres to beloved athletes like George Foreman. I was speaking and presenting to thousands of people each year and I had won pretty much every fitness accolade there was to win. I was teaching to packed classes throughout NYC and I had even been on the back of a Special K cereal box. In my field these were meaningful accomplishments. Yet none of it was ever good enough for me.

My inner critic would remind me every day that I was not quite enough. I was a fraud, she kept telling me, an imposter, and one day I would be found out. The more I tried to ignore this voice, the louder she got and the more she chipped away at my self-esteem and confidence.

She would never let me forget that my father was an alcoholic and everyone around me knew it. She always reminded me that my dance teachers thought I would never amount to much. And she never failed to send me reminders that the choreographer I worshiped thought I needed to lose weight. My inner critic seemed to thrive when I was about to find the courage to begin dancing with my life. Just as I was about to be gifted with an incredible opportunity, the voices of my past that reminded me I was too fat, too stupid, or just not enough would speak up.

Eventually my perfectionism led to anxiety, which courted me as a constant companion. While at first my symptoms were subtle and easy to hide, they slowly grew into full-blown panic attacks. As with any perfectionist, I tried to manage my symptoms perfectly—the trouble was that while I could hide my racing heart, the tightening of my chest, and my rushing thoughts of how could I leave the room without anyone noticing—I could not hide my last symptom, which was an instant full-body sweat. This was uncomfortable, extremely embarrassing, and more public proof of just how imperfect I was. After every panic attack I felt drained, lost, sad, exhausted, lonely, and even more imperfect.

As my panic attacks became more frequent my calendar began to empty out. For two years, I turned down high-profile work such as appearances on the *Today* show, *The View*, and *CBS This Morning* out of fear that I would lose control as my anxiety and panic attacks took over. The only thing I knew at that time that I could do perfectly was have a full-blown panic attack—I just never knew when or where it was going to happen. The tighter my grasp for control, the more I felt it slipping entirely out of my hands.

I knew then that just as surely as my calendar was going to go blank, my life was going to continue to shrink unless I got to the bottom of my problem. I spent seven-plus years in therapy dedicated to overcoming my anxiety, therapy which at the start was also supplemented by prescription medication; I studied the best literature and research on the subject; I completed a positive psychology program led by author and Harvard University lecturer Tal Ben-Shahar; and I have tried and tested many strategies in my laboratory of life. These along with my professional experience and insights into the healing powers of physical movement were the raw material that became the Perfection Detox Program. I knew that others could use the lessons that

I learned to help them eliminate their own perfectionistic tendencies. What I didn't expect was how high the number of these women would be.

TWENTY-ONE STEPS TO BREAKING FREE FROM PERFECTIONISM

I suspect that perfection has wreaked havoc on your life as it had on mine. The only difference between you and me right now is that I have lived on both sides of the condition. It took me seven years to untangle, deconstruct, and wrestle my doubt demons to the sidelines, but once I did my life expanded in ways beyond my wildest imagination.

My intention with this book is to share with you the best tools and strategies from my own journey to help you fast track your path to a life of joy and freedom. In this book, you will find my seven-year process of detoxing from perfectionism compressed into just twenty-one steps.

I know how limited your time is and how many things you have on your to-do list, so I thought the best way for us to become acquainted was to give you the Cliff's Notes version for the journey ahead. I have tried to make this book as efficient as possible, without short-changing you on the how and why of each step.

The twenty-one Perfection Detox instructions are divided into three parts, each of which has a distinct focus and intended outcome. Here's what they look like:

Part One: Tame Your Inner Critic and Explore Your Potential. In this section, you will uncover the negative voices of your past and discover whom they belong to. You will also dissect and release any limiting beliefs that have allowed perfectionism to move into the driver's seat of your life.

Part Two: Shift Your Focus and Live Bravely. This is where you will discover how to reclaim your true self and remember the good of who you are. By shifting your focus away from the negative voices of your inner critic to the positive focus of a life well lived, you will create a strong and healthy foundation from which to build your best future.

Part Three: Liberate Yourself and Unleash Your Joy. Part Three sets the stage for your abundant future. It is designed to short-circuit your doubt demons and hardwire your mental state to one of optimal joy, positivity, and potential.

Even though, as mentioned above, perfectionists share a lot of the same internal struggles, everyone's perfectionism is unique, and there is no one-size-fits-all solution.

With this notion in mind, I've designed this program to allow you to focus on the areas of your life most affected. While I do recommend that you complete all twenty-one steps, aim to finish as many of them as you can. You might find that some of the steps speak to you more than others—and you should be sure to spend more time on the ones that hit your own perfectionistic nerve.

The program is designed to be completed in a sequential order. Based on the science of positive psychology, my life lab, and the thousands of hours I have spent teaching this material, this detox is built on a methodology that will allow you to drive out perfectionism without disrupting your day-to-day life. That being said, you know your story, your struggles, and your most tender pain points. This is your journey, and your intuition will be one of your greatest guides throughout this detox. If any of the steps do not resonate with you, feel free to skip them and perhaps revisit at a later time.

THERE IS NO PERFECT WAY TO DO THIS

While there are twenty-one steps, this does not mean the program needs to be completed in twenty-one days. For some of you, it may be the perfect match. One step per day, one section per week, three weeks and you are done. For others, it will be a less compact process. You may breeze through a few steps and then find one that you want to sit with for a while. Take as long as you need, try each one on for size and then, just like a good friend, you will find certain steps will be your best companion at different times of your life.

I encourage you to take what works, stay with what works well, and remember this is not a race but a dance. A dance that spirals inwards and leads you back to the person you were before perfection cast its ugly spell on you.

I have seven steps that I recommend for success with the detox:

1. Complete each step in the order that they appear.
2. If a step does not resonate with you, leave it and come back to it at another time.
3. If a step feels particularly useful or rewarding, play with it for as long as you like before moving on.

4. Stay curious during the detox and welcome the revelations about yourself.
5. Some days you will rock the detox and some days just showing up will be enough.
6. Do your best, and that will be perfect.
7. The perfect time to start is now.

A Recommendation Before You Dive In

I also invite you to keep a journal nearby as you work your way through the detox. Throughout the book, I will be asking you to write down your thoughts, feelings, and new ideas. While we have all gotten used to taking notes on our computers and smartphones, to maximize your time and ramp up your results, nothing is as powerful as pen and paper when it comes to self-reflection.

Go out and get yourself a journal you love, something that feels good when you touch it or catches your eye or makes you smile when you see it. There's been a lot of research about the benefits of keeping a journal, including that which showed that journaling can help reduce intrusive thoughts and improve memory.

When and how you use your journal is up to you. There is no perfect time to journal and no perfect way to write. Some days you may find yourself writing a few pages and others just a few sentences. Perhaps some days you just don't feel like writing at all and that is perfectly fine.

While I don't see you or your fellow perfectionists embracing the idea of journaling at work, I do suggest that you jot down triggers and thoughts into your smartphone as they come up throughout the day. Then, whenever it feels right to you, pick up your journal and write your thoughts, observations, and reflections in more detail.

IT'S TIME TO LIVE THE LIFE YOU DESERVE

Here's the absolute truth: You deserve a life filled with joy, hope, and possibility. If you have picked up this book, you know deep down that you are yearning for this life yet to be lived, with fear diminished, anxiety and regret reduced, and optimism restored.

My hope is that this book will be a resource that you come back to again and again. Whether you have a lazy afternoon (we can dream, right?) or just five minutes before an important meeting, this is your handbook for taming your inner critic, living bravely, and unleashing your joy.

Have confidence in this process and trust the moments as they unfold. Lastly, before we begin, I invite you to place three ingredients into your heart. These are: Acceptance, Love, and Courage. Acceptance will help balance your judgment, Love will manage your fear, and Courage will help soothe your anxiety.

With *The Perfection Detox,* you will finally be able to release the fear that is rooted in perfectionism and soar into a life of your dreams. And as Elizabeth Gilbert said, "Perfectionism is just fear in really good shoes." Now is the time to take off the fancy footwear and step into the life that is waiting for you.

TAME YOUR INNER CRITIC
AND EXPLORE YOUR POTENTIAL

PART ONE

Noticing the Noise

I F YOU'VE EVER TRIED TO MEDITATE, YOU KNOW THAT IT'S INCREDIBLY DIFFICULT TO ACHIEVE A "quiet" mind. No matter how hard you try to focus on your breath, there are those pesky thoughts determined to break into your consciousness . . . "Oh no—I forgot to pick up my dry cleaning, what am I going to wear to the party?!" "I can't believe I overslept this morning, when am I going to find time to prep for my meeting?" "Is it my turn to do school pick up today, I think I remember Sara mentioning she needed to switch her day?"

While it may not appear so, this inner chatter is not frivolous. It's part of the internal monologue we all have that in large part shapes our sense of who we are. I'm not referring to the part of the thought thoroughfare that's congested with trivial to-do traffic, but the deeper, more consequential dispatches that impact your identity. The ones that tell you you're not good enough or smart enough or *perfect* enough; the ones that echo deep-seated insecurities, perhaps entrenched long ago. Powerful messages of this sort are there, whether you realize it or not, and they must be deciphered and dismantled if you want to live bravely and unleash your joy.

In this first step, we're going to turn our focus to this inner chatter and work on identifying your top three negative thoughts that seem to play on repeat. I'll help guide you first toward awareness of what your internal monologue is saying to you, and then later we'll work on replacing the self-destructive messages. But before we get into that process, I want to give you a little glimpse into what goes on in your mind each day.

A DAY IN THE LIFE OF YOUR MIND

Researchers at the Laboratory of Neuro Imaging at the University of Southern California have determined that you have about 70,000 thoughts per day, or approximately 48.6 thoughts per minute. And a whopping 95 percent of the thoughts you'll have today will be the same as those you had yesterday. (Some people say that these kinds of stats are impossible to prove, but I suspect there's a lot of truth to these figures.)

This wouldn't mean much if the thoughts were neutral, but they're not: 80 percent of our habitual thoughts are negative in tone. This is not a character flaw, but an evolutionary, self-preservation device dating to our first days on earth, when the ability to detect a threat could mean the difference between staying alive or becoming dinner.

The challenge, and why this detox is imperative for your health and happiness, is that your brain cannot tell the difference between your perception of a situation and the reality. Your internal chemical response will be exactly the same whether you have a thought that makes you feel anxious, such as, "They are going to find out that I am not as smart as my resume suggests" or you have a hungry animal chasing you down the street (side note: if this happens, you may want to consider moving). In either case, your body will be flooded by a quick release of adrenaline and cortisol and transported into full-blown stress mode.

For perfectionists, the predisposition toward negativity can be especially destructive because it feeds on our insecurities, creating an airtight loop of doubt and self-criticism. Unchallenged, repeated negative thoughts become the joy-stealing monsters that cloud our perception of ourselves, our relationships, and our expectations. They affect most aspects of our lives, snuffing out dreams, deflating desires, and keeping us from reaching our potential, which, in an ironic twist, is what the perfectionist yearns for more than anything else.

For most of us, the doubt demons have grown so powerful that we don't even notice how they've positioned themselves into the driver's seat of our lives. We think we are in charge of our journey, but we are not. They are. It's time to take back the control.

GRABBING YOUR BRAIN BY THE REINS

How do you take back control from your doubt demons? You learn to stop fueling them with the chewy negativity chatter they love so much. You learn how to detox from false, defeatist thoughts and how to introduce refreshing, restorative, positive thoughts that will reinforce productive self-perceptions. You can think of this as you would a move (minus the physical labor)—you're going to pack up and move out the negative thoughts, creating space for a new and upgraded way of thinking to move in.

It's also important to "move out" the meaning you've given to these thoughts. Thoughts have no power until we give them meaning, especially those we've used to construct the mirage of perfection. After all, *perfect* is really nothing more than an illusion that's self-conjured and socially reinforced.

For many of my clients and the women I work with in my workshops, common negativity triggers revolve around appearance, work, relationship expectations, and aging. The women, especially working mothers, often describe the preponderance of repetitive thoughts about not being enough—at home, at work, or socially. Their thoughts carry a punishing tone of guilt and dissatisfaction that saps them of energy and optimism about the future. What they don't realize, and what I help reveal to them, is that instead of allowing space for change, growth, and expansion in our lives, these thoughts suffocate and shut out little opportunities our daily lives present. They prevent us from finding the extraordinary in the seemingly ordinary.

For many years, my top three persistent negative thoughts revolved around the themes of criticism, comparison, and control. While they vary depending upon the scenario, they usually sound something like this:

1. I am not smart enough to be up on this stage. Someone is going to ask me something I don't know and they will see me for the fraud that I am.
2. My body is not perfect and as I am a fitness expert it should be perfect.
3. I can't believe I made that mistake—they are going to think I am an idiot and that I don't belong in this meeting.

These types of thoughts became so reflexive that I wouldn't even consider them as factors in the emotional pain I was experiencing. Learning how to detox from these negative thoughts was a pivotal step in my recovery from perfectionism.

People who have attended my workshops shared other common themes in their top three hits. The Imposter Syndrome is probably the biggest underlying ruminating thought. Here are just a few examples:

1. "Who am I to be doing this?" "I am going to be found out." "People are going to know I really don't have all the answers and certainly I don't know everything."
2. "I'm a fraud and everyone is just waiting for me to make a mistake to prove that I didn't deserve this promotion, job, etc."
3. "I can't believe I just ran into my boss without my makeup on and in sweats. She just saw the real me and I bet it is not what she wants for her team."
4. "I have to look perfect, say the perfect thing, manage the room perfectly, and make sure everyone is happy for this to be a good party/experience."

If you are not sure which thoughts are your joy-stealing monsters, spend today listening more carefully to the words and phrases you use when talking to yourself (please tell me you also talk to yourself?). If you use the word *should* a little too often in evaluating yourself or others, it is a good indicator that you are operating on presumptions that may be cumulatively more toxic than helpful.

When you jump to negative conclusions about yourself, other people, or situations by saying things like "I'll never do that again," Or, "I wish that . . ." it is another clue that a thought detox is needed. If you make a mistake and see only the mistake, you might need a more forgiving reality check. Start to write down a list of these types of thoughts in your journal and look for patterns.

SORTING THROUGH TODAY'S THOUGHT TORNADO

Some people I've worked with have had difficulty determining if a thought was popping up just because they were having a bad day or if indeed it was a top three hit. And here's what I had to say to them: "When in doubt, go with the thoughts that feel right to you in the moment and know that you can always revamp your focus at any time." In other words, there are no wrong answers. It's important to remember that this step, or any step for that matter, does not have to be done perfectly—you will not be graded or judged on your Perfection Detox performance.

Another factor that can make it a bit tricky to identify your top three thoughts is the presence of multiple voices in your head. I'm not referring to multiple *personalities*, but voices—the different ones you may use when you're talking to a friend or family member, your significant other, your child, or yourself. The degree of compassion, patience, sternness, and so on will undoubtedly vary in each case.

In one workshop that I ran, a woman named Diane acknowledged this variation in voice was affecting her ability to determine her self-directed thoughts. Diane told me that at first she had some difficulty sorting out which were her top hits. She wrote: "I seem to have two voices in my head. One is negative, judgmental, and mean, and the other is kind, gentle, sweet, and accepting."

By going through the Perfection Detox, Diane was able to realize that the negative voice was indicative of how she spoke to herself and the more positive voice was the kinder, gentler one that she used to talk to others. She described this first voice as being part of her "inner, more secretive dialogue" that she "hid from the world." It took going into this dark, hidden dialogue for Diane to find her doubt demons. And you will likely need to take this trip, too, to get to your true top hits.

For all of us, our top hits flow through the inner dialogue that we keep to ourselves, and it's partly due to this secrecy that recurring negative thoughts have so much power. The moment we shine a light on our hits, their power begins to diminish (they grow even weaker when we achieve acceptance, but we'll get to that in Step 6). I call them "hits" because that is exactly what happens each time these thoughts bounce around our minds unnoticed and unmanaged. Just like the popular song you keep hearing on the radio becomes an "earworm" our negative thoughts can become a repeating loop in our mind. The difference being that one lifts you up and the other pulls you down. With each negative thought, a blow is leveled at your heart and a piece of your self-esteem is chipped away. Thought by thought, blow by blow, you are knocking down your confidence and courage.

Your top hits may change as you become more aware of them. While different thoughts may flit in and out of your consciousness there will probably be one that you latch onto faster than others. This is your keystone thought.

Just as we have good and bad habits we also have good and bad thoughts. As discussed by Charles Duhigg in *The Power of Habit*, creating new habits often revolves around a keystone habit, the one action that has a ripple effect on all the others and has the power to transform your life. Just like our habits we have a keystone thought that has the power to transform our life, for better or worse. The more powerful the thought the more powerful the impact. The trouble is that negative thoughts pack more punch than the positive, and if left unmanaged will fire up your perfectionistic tendencies and wreak havoc with your mind and mood.

As you know one of my top three hits was that I should be smarter. This turned out to also be my keystone thought. Same thought, just a different disguise. As the stakes became higher (which they will as you become braver), it would keep popping up.

During my three-decade career as a fitness expert, I would often need to attend high-stakes meetings when I was auditioning for a position as a spokesperson or interviewing to be a part of an advisory board. As much as I was not a fan of these types of meetings, I had finally gotten my inner critic under control and no longer allowed my self-doubt to overwhelm me.

But as I transitioned out of fitness and into my new career as a motivational speaker and writer, the landscape changed, the stakes became higher and my darn doubt demons decided to make an appearance.

It was a hot summer day in New York City and a few weeks earlier my good friend Dorie Clark, who also happens to be incredibly smart (Harvard smart) and the author of several books, had invited me to a writer's dinner. In my mind I was not yet officially an author as I was still in the proposal stage of this book, but this was of no concern to Dorie. She simply thought the dinner would be a great opportunity for me to meet some other writers who lived in the city, and so I agreed to go.

It just so happened that along with the authors' dinner, the hottest day of the summer arrived. I had been feeling a little anxious but managed to keep it in check until it was time to decide what I was going to wear. My doubt demons began to rear their ugly heads and positioned themselves on the sofa as though they were judges on a reality show called *What Not to Wear If You Want to Fit In*.

That evening's dinner could have been attended by authors, speakers, teachers, moms, or just about anyone who was not in the world of fitness. I had learned how to fit in with a fitness crowd, but this was new territory for me, and so was really comfortable terrain for my inner critic.

I decided to walk to the restaurant as to get a cab at rush hour would be impossible and the subway was like a toaster oven. As I slowly turned the corner to the street where the restaurant was, I saw a few people that I recognized from my social media feed and knew they were writers. They had all stopped to greet each other before going inside, and as they filtered through the front door, my doubt demons saw this as the perfect time to pounce. "They look so smart . . . of course they are writers, probably academia, and they all know each other. You know, you really should have gone back to school for your Ph.D. before starting this book. They all fit in so well and look at you with your newly bleached blond hair . . . you are going to stand out like a sore thumb. Look at how well dressed they are! Why did you decide to wear that long dress today? I told you the black pants would have made you look smarter *and* thinner. They are obviously published authors, probably *New York Times* bestsellers . . . what on earth made you think you would fit in?"

Phew. Doesn't it exhaust you just to read?! My head swam with these rapid-fire thoughts for the next few moments. In the past, the stream would have continued until I had reached the table where everyone was seated and it would have prevented me from being present and being able to enjoy the evening. However, as a recovered perfectionist, I can now recognize my analytical and self-demeaning demons for the frauds they are. I knew Dorie would not have invited me if she thought I would not fit into the mix, and I knew that any of her friends would be gracious, supportive, and welcoming. By the time I reached the front door of the restaurant, I had shut the demons down and was ready to have a great time. And as a side note to my inner critic, who on earth in their right mind would wear black pants on a sweltering hot day in the city?

Daily Detox

1. The first thing I'll ask you to do here is to identify three of your most common recurring thoughts that are negative in tone. Begin to scan your thoughts, using a lens of gentle observation, not judgment, to take stock of their focus, tone, even volume. As you do this, recurring thoughts and themes will start to reveal themselves and you will be given the opportunity to envision an alternative and healthier attitude. Keep in mind that our goal for now is simply awareness and nothing more.

   You might notice your thoughts immediately—they'll be the ones raising their hands yelling "pick me, pick me"—or if you're like Diane, your thoughts will be subtler in nature or hidden in the depths of your inner dialogue. In this case, I recommend that you spend twenty-four hours jotting down thoughts that seem to pop up repeatedly. You may be questioning if you have any, but trust me they are there. It is only because they have become so embedded in your psyche that they have gone unnoticed for so long. It is time to shake them up and move them out.

   As you review your list of thoughts, consider which three resonate most deeply, feel the most familiar, and sting a little. The approach for dealing with these thoughts need not be complicated. Simply ask yourself, has the thought added or diminished my sense of joy from the day? If this feels uncomfortable, this is likely a sign that you've landed on the persistent thoughts that pain you the most. Eventually you will learn to make them less toxic by reframing them and releasing them. Then, you will have made space for the thoughts that fuel your dreams versus those that starve them.

   Once you have your top three negative hits down on paper, do not judge them, label them, or ruminate on them (pinky promise!). Also, a gentle reminder to write no more than three top hits. You can change the thoughts you want to work with whenever you like, but never more than three at a time. If you have already pinpointed one thought, your keystone thought, feel free to work with just that one for now.

If at this point you have been able to isolate the thoughts that are separating you from your joy, feel free to move on to step two. However, if you are having a difficult time uncovering your negative thoughts, continue on with this daily detox.

2. "Watch your thoughts, they become words; watch your words, they become actions; watch your actions, they become habits; watch your habits, they become character; watch your character, for it becomes your destiny." This quote has been attributed to everyone from Lao Tzu to Margaret Thatcher and Frank Outlaw. No matter the source, it's particularly relevant to this step.

Some of my clients have found that focusing on their repetitive actions is easier than pinpointing the thoughts themselves. Over the next day or so, pay attention to—and even start jotting down in your journal—the actions that you take that seem to produce negative outcomes. Then, see if you can trace the actions back to the originating thoughts and ideas. If they were driven by negative feelings—insecurity, fear, or regret—these may be the recurrent negative thoughts that keep festering and showing up through misguided actions.

You might look at this call for observation and find it impractical, or wonder how you're supposed to be both living your life *and* observing it. Just do the best you can with what you have in front of you. Some days you will catch a negative thought and have time to jot down a quick observation, other days you may go hours before noticing the compounding effect of negative triggers, and some days will be such a whirlwind of putting out fires and staying afloat in this journey called life, that you may not have time to even think about the detox until the end of your day. This is all good. Just the simple, yet profound act of becoming aware that you are ready to disconnect from the illusion called perfection is a fantastic beginning.

3. Your mind and body can become great allies if you learn to listen to your inner wisdom. Your breath is a terrific tool to help you recognize a trigger thought that could be a top three hit.

With that in mind, I want you to begin to check in with your breathing throughout your day. If your breath is deep and fluid, it means you are relaxed and in your power. However, if you find yourself holding your breath or it suddenly becomes short and shallow, it is likely you have been sideswiped by a negative thought. A smaller breath means you are becoming smaller, taking up less space and shutting down. Sitting is one of the worst positions for both your breathing and mindset.

The following is a simple breath exercise that you can do anytime you need to tap into your inner guide and wisdom. This exercise can be done standing or seated, in shoes or barefoot.

Begin by placing both feet on the floor, hip distance apart.

Imagine there is a golden string attached to the crown of your head and it is gently pulling you upwards. Try to lengthen your spine and move your shoulders, so they stack over your hips.

Once settled, place one hand on your chest and the other on your abdomen. To begin, simply draw your attention to your breath and observe which hand is moving more. Most likely it will be your top hand indicating that you are breathing from your chest.

Take the next few breaths to observe with a sense of curiosity your normal way of breathing. After a few moments, slowly begin to deepen your breath. Think of filling your entire body with energizing air, so much so, that your top hand becomes still and your lower hand begins to move in and out with each inhale and exhale.

When you breathe deeply from your belly instead of the traditional shallow chest breathing that we all tend to do, your breath acts as a bridge between your brain and your body. If you find it challenging to read this as you try to practice, this exercise is also available for you at theperfectiondetox.com as an audio download.

Today is about heightening your awareness and waking up to your life. This is the moment you begin to tame your inner critic and reclaim your power.

Starve Your Doubt Demons

W E'VE ESTABLISHED THAT YOUR TOP THREE HITS ARE MORE LIKELY TO BE NEGATIVE IN nature, often reflecting what you perceive to be your shortcomings, failures, or lapses. For most of us, our brains have become so conditioned to ponder, mull over, and dissect these pieces of information that we are not even conscious that it is happening. Yet, whether we're aware of it or not, this constant and subliminal stream of negative thinking can have a devastating effect both on our emotional and physical well-being.

When we begin to spiral into revolutions of repetitive thoughts we are now caught up in the toxic and powerful current of rumination. Instead of using our mind as a gateway for insight and learning, we become trapped in a box of limiting thoughts, which left alone long enough will become our new belief system.

When this is your headspace, you're hard-pressed to see the good, especially in yourself (I've heard it said—and think it's a great analogy—that in this state negativity sticks to us like Velcro, while positivity slides off us like Teflon). Even when the opportunity for positivity presents itself we often default to devaluing and minimizing it. For example, think about the last time someone paid you a compliment; my guess is that you brushed it aside. Yet when something negative does arise we tend to exaggerate both the cause and the effect.

Negativity needs nourishment to survive and thrive—but here's the good news: you have the power to cut off the food supply. The key is to recognize and disarm thoughts and thought loops before they become ruminations, repetitive rehashings of events or experiences that are infinitely unresolvable because they've occurred in the past. The habit of rumination will only move you deeper into perfectionistic paralysis and further away from your powerful potential.

THE RUSE OF RUMINATION

Rumination is the soul-sucking process of trying to change what does not exist. The past is over and the future is out of our control, yet there is a piece of our brain that believes that, "If I think about this long enough, hard enough, and often enough, the situation will change and I will feel better." We are waiting to change how we feel, by trying to change the past or control the future. I don't need to tell you how futile this is. Our power can only be found in the present moment. We give away our power, over and over again, each time we obsess about the past or worry about the future.

Experts in the psychology field began calling this habit "rumination" because the act of repetitive thinking is similar to the regurgitation of cud by "ruminant" animals such as goats, sheep, or cows (if that image is not enough to make you want to retrain your brain, I am not sure what is). This means every time we ruminate, we are slowly chewing over what has already been partially swallowed. While flipping through a magazine recently I came across the heading, "Be sure to taste your words before you spit them out." I would change that to say, "Be sure to taste your thoughts before you chew on them."

Research on psychological stressors has shown rumination to be more damaging than self-blame as it relates to our well-being and happiness. This is according to the largest online test on stress ever done in the United Kingdom, which gathered responses from over thirty-two thousand participants from 172 countries, and also showed repetitive thinking as one of the biggest predicators of depression, anxiety, and stress.

Catching ourselves when we ruminate on negative thoughts is a powerful tool because it enables us to release the passive role of judgment and inaction. It is not that hard to catch yourself ruminating about an experience that involves someone else. What is harder to notice but is even more toxic to our emotional well-being is self-focused rumination.

Self-focused rumination is what happens when we get hooked on negative thoughts about ourselves. We obsess over our own shortcomings, missteps, and perceived wrongdoing. We become our own devil's advocate, pointing out our flaws but neglecting to offer up any solutions.

Susan Nolen-Hoeksema, former professor of psychology at Yale University, and Sonja Lyubomirsky, Ph.D., author of *The How of Happiness*, researched this phenomenon. They came to the conclusion that self-focused rumination breeds negatively biased thinking, makes us feel worse, saps motivation, increases the risk of depression, and actually impairs us from solving the problem that caused this feeling in the first place. This is why it is critical to become aware of the negative thoughts that spin us into a toxic loop of disruptive thinking. It is only when we are aware that we can then take positive action to move us forward and upward.

I can sense when I drop into self-focused rumination when I notice a subtle shift in my mood. Without exception, if my brain latches onto one of my top three hits and refuses to let go, I soon find myself becoming annoyed and agitated. Small things will start to bother me, my stomach will feel tense and anxious, and I stop seeing the good in my day. If left unmanaged, I will begin to feel a little blue or depressed (just like the research says). As a normally optimistic person, this is my alarm bell. My body alerts me to the fact that my subconscious has begun latching on to a self-directed negative thought or two. Instead of seeing it for what it is, letting it go and moving on, my brain and body have now become caught up in the rope of self-focused rumination, and it always pulls me into the land of doubt and destruction.

If logically we know ruminating is bad for our health and happiness, why is it so hard to stop? Just like a bad habit that we know is not helping us move toward our goals and dreams, why oh why is it so hard to quit?

Eric Zimmer, host of *The One You Feed* podcast, gives a fantastic analogy: "Think of it like taking a walk in the woods. Your thoughts are like hikers. The first hiker has to blaze her own trail, but over subsequent trips a trail gets worn into the ground and more and more hikers will take that trail. The more hikers that take the trail the clearer it becomes and the more likely that future hikers will take it. It takes much more energy to go off the trail."

Our brain wants to be as efficient as possible in its energy output. As our brains' default is the negative, the negative thoughts take up less energy and so are more likely to go onto the rinse and repeat cycle. Repetition creates mastery and the more we repeat the negative thoughts the more power they will have over us. The problem is that when our ideas repeat often enough they also create a physiological response. Think about anything hard enough and often enough, your body will need to adapt to protect itself from that onslaught of negativity. The physiological response will more than likely be fight or flight mode. More cortisol, more adrenaline, and more stress.

For many of us rumination has become a habit, and as with any habit rumination can also have triggers. Charles Duhigg, *New York Times* business reporter and the author of *The Power of Habit*, writes that the creation of a habit can be broken down into three parts, also known as a habit loop:

1. The trigger
2. The habit
3. The reward

Just like habits, when we ruminate we are often triggered subliminally by a cue. This cue could be one of five things:

1. Location
2. Time
3. Emotional state
4. Other people
5. The action immediately before the habit

The cues may change but one of my big ones became a location: the shower. If I was not fully present, I could find myself getting ready for my day in a super bad mood and not knowing why. Rumination loves inactivity of the brain and so the shower had become the perfect location for my brain to notice it could go unnoticed. Bathing takes very little concentration and so my shower became the location for my idle brain to lather up my negativity. Ten minutes later, as I toweled off I also realized I was pissed off, not a great way to start my day. As soon as I realized that the shower was a trigger, I created a new positive action and began using my shower as my morning mindfulness ritual. As let's be honest, not showering was hardly an option.

RESTORE THE POWER OF CHOICE WITH POSITIVE NOURISHMENT

The perfectionist's tendency to default to the familiar (yet unproductive) comfort of rumination can be costly. While it's not expensive in the way that, say, a shoe shopping habit is, you pay by sacrificing your power of choice—which comes at a decidedly higher price. When we surrender the power of choice, we have planted ourselves firmly in the passenger's seat of our own lives. Negative thinking takes the wheel and we can't see options beyond our negativity bias.

We have the power to shorten or elongate our suffering based upon which thoughts we cling to. Unless you begin to switch your focus over to something good, lasting change will not be possible. Science has shown that simply trying to erase a negative thought is not an effective solution. Think back to the last time someone told you not to focus on something, where did your focus go? Remember that time you were out for dinner and your friend said don't look behind you. All you wanted to do throughout dessert was turn around. You say don't and your brain wants to do the exact opposite.

Our brain does not like a vacuum, and so as we clear out the negative it is important to fill the space with something positive. If we neglect to do a follow-up action, that space will be filled by our default programming, another negative thought. For many of the women I work with, a follow-up action that is easy to implement is to quietly and kindly remind themselves that they are enough. By simply refusing to be at war with themselves, they create a solid foundation from which to begin their journey back to joy.

OUT WITH RUMINATION, IN WITH REFLECTION

Rumination is different from reflection. Reflection allows us to see the past for what it was versus what we wished it had been. When we hook onto a thought and become so tightly committed to only reliving our perceived mistakes, we miss the potential to uncover the useful data that lies within both the hit and the miss.

Just because we go through an imperfect experience does not mean there is not usable and important information to be found. When we are in a place of self-reflection we are better able to data mine the positive. The thoughts will be more neutral and action-oriented in tone, created around an inner dialogue stemming from open-ended questions such as "What can I learn from this?" Reflection allows us to carry forward what is working, and leave the rest behind.

To be our best and to optimize our potential it is important to learn from our past so we can prepare for the future. However there is a wide gap between rumination (self-punishment) and reflection (self-discovery) when it comes to improving our results.

Below is a chart that you can use to see in which state you tend to spend more of your time. Both take up a lot of headspace, but only reflection will uncover new information and solutions that will fuel your future for the better.

Rumination Mindset	**Reflection Mindset**
Thinks about the past	Resides in the present
Wishes for a different outcome	Works with reality
Fills in the blanks with stories	Works with the facts
Uses the lens of self-judgment	Uses the lens of self-compassion
Problem-focused	Solution-focused
Views challenges as threats	Views challenges as opportunities
Paralyzed by problems	Takes action
Doubt demons thrive	Doubt demons starve

Your brain has spent years defaulting to the practice of repetitive thinking so be patient with yourself. Think of this step as a dance between awareness and acceptance. The more curiosity and self-compassion you can apply to the process the more enjoyable the dance will be.

Daily Detox

1. Rumination is a habit and that is why it can be so hard to catch as it gains traction in your mind. The first step is to watch for your rumination triggers and write them down. Is it a place, perhaps at the gym, in front of a mirror, or when you drop your kids off at school? Is it when you are around certain people? Perhaps you find yourself shifting into comparison mode, and the spin cycle of self-doubt begins around certain work colleagues. Maybe it is when you are tired, since our willpower and "won't power" are less available to us at the end of a long day.

   When you spot your triggers, write them down. Then, begin a practice of avoiding and/or eliminating as many as possible. Sometimes changing up your regular routine will be enough. When it is not possible to remove or avoid a trigger completely, create a new and positive response in place of rumination. Even the act of putting a plan in place is a huge step in the right direction. For example, if one of your triggers is the mirror, as it is for many women, while it probably is not practical to avoid mirrors completely, we can create a healthier and upgraded response to our reflection.

   On the days you find yourself wanting to pick yourself apart, can you start a new healthy habit to stop the negative trigger from kicking into high gear? One that has worked for many of the women I work with is to create a mini mantra or find a power word to immediately shift the direction of their inner dialogue. One of the words I use is "pineapple." Saying my power word allows me to notice that my brain is about to spiral into the negative, "pineapple" always makes me smile and it immediately shuts the rumination trigger down. Perhaps for you it is looking at your reflection and learning to smile, or quietly saying, "hush now" as you begin to hear the voice of your inner critic. These are small but powerful reframes that will move your focus away from what could be a potentially heart-destroying interaction.

Susan Nolen-Hoeksema's definition of rumination is repeatedly and passively thinking about the causes or consequences of problems without moving into active problem solving. You, my friend, are already moving from thinking to doing.

2. When we ruminate, our mind has become full yet we are far from being mindful.

Practice a mantra to help break the rumination cycle. One of my favorites, which also resonates with people in my workshops and presentations, is "Be here now." It's simple, but works like a snap of the fingers on repetitive thoughts. Repeat it as often as needed until you've silenced your internal critic. Another one I like to use is "I am enough." More recently I have shifted my mantra to "I refuse to beat myself up."

3. Research out of Rutgers University is showing that mindfulness and physical activity, also known as MAP training, can have a positive effect on rumination. During my years as a dancer the one place I never ruminated was in class or on stage. When my body was in motion, I became fully present and my mind became still. For a quick fix during your day, simply S.T.O.P.: **S**tand up. **T**ake a walk. **O**bserve your surroundings. **P**ick a positive thought. The first two actions get you moving, the third pulls you into the present, and the last step makes sure you are filling the gap with positive reinforcement. A change of scenery can be just the trick to disrupt your thoughts and change your mind. If you don't have time to take a walk, tap your feet. Anything that gets you up and your body moving will work.

STEP 3

Get the Weight off Your Shoulders

WHEN PERFECTIONISTS (ESPECIALLY WOMEN) THINK ABOUT "WEIGHT" IT TENDS TO BE THE kind that can be measured on a scale, that is, the weight we carry on our skeletal frames. This weight has the potential to propel us into feelings of regret, anguish, and self-loathing—a response that we'll address later in the book. For now, however, I want us to focus on a different kind of weight: the metaphorical weight of perfectionism that you carry on your shoulders.

The weight of perfectionism is a heavy burden, yet you're probably not even aware that it's there. In the same way that we don't notice the pounds creeping onto our bodies until our clothes don't quite fit, the weight of perfection can sneak up on us. We tend not to notice it dragging us down until we stop deriving pleasure from our relationship with life, or until our relationships cease to find joy through us. Suddenly, we feel as if our lives don't quite fit, or as if we don't fit our lives.

Of course, the question is how does the burden grow? It doesn't increase by way of excess calories or reduced exercise, but instead as layers of unmet expectations built in breadth and height. Expectation is a big feature in the life of a perfectionist: We expect a lot from ourselves and will push toward our goals—at whatever cost, even when they are unreasonable, unattainable, and perhaps not in our best interest.

In addition, if you are someone who expects those around you to be perfect (more about this in Step 15), these expectations will also be cast out onto other people. The presumption in this case is that naturally all people would want to be as perfect as you are, and you project upon them inflexible expectations for excellence in all things.

You might also believe that the same rules and sense of obligation that guide you guide others. Yet, this is normally an illusion, one that can grow into a bottomless pit of disappointment and potentially derail existing relationships or prevent budding ones from fully developing. Imagine the weight we unwittingly place upon friends, co-workers, and family when they feel the only outcome good enough to satisfy our exceptionally high standards is the perfect one.

In this step, I want to help open your eyes to the level of expectation that exists in your life and the weight it places on you and others around you. When you detox from the expectation that life is perfect and move your attention off the outcome and onto the experience, you can undergo a profound transformation and derive more joy from your days. This is not about giving less effort, but it is about changing the expectations you attach to your performance at home, at work, and in life.

NOT-SO-GREAT EXPECTATIONS

Expectations have been defined as beliefs that (1) something will happen or be the case in the future or that (2) someone will or should achieve something. On paper, they don't sound particularly bad or burdensome, but run them through a perfectionist's mind and a different story will emerge. To the perfectionist, "expectations are resentments under construction," as the author Anne Lamott once wrote. This is true whether we're talking about the expectations we put upon ourselves or the ones we project onto others; in either case, it does not take long for those resentments to build up and become psychically burdensome.

Expectation is a flawed model to live by for both our happiness and productivity. We unwittingly set up expectations, thinking that they will increase our output and productivity, maybe our likability and success too, but all we are doing is creating unrelenting standards and barriers that set us up for failure.

As a perfectionist, you are probably hypersensitive to what may or may not be expected of you. The problem is that more often than not these expectations are not just unrealistic, but also separate us from the reality of the experience.

Unrealistic expectations are often self-defined and likely to be both inflexible and cause more harm than good. They work a little like silent mini contracts that we set up with ourselves, the terms being forever *not* in our favor as they establish a need to know it all and control it all (impossibilities) and to never relent in our pursuit of perfection. And if you're like me, you up the ante and elevate the expectation each time, pushing the reality of meeting your own expectations further and further out of reach. This is a perpetual setup for failure and disappointment.

Perfectionists are constantly conjuring up unrealistic expectations that are often self-made and devoid of reality. You might recognize them in a scenario such as this: *I know with absolute certainty that the other moms will be bringing homemade cookies to the school party; it's better for me to stay up until one in the morning making them, than to pick up something from the store and be the only one not showing up with something made by hand.*

It can be reassuring to discover that you're not alone in these fabrications. In a recent interview, best-selling author Simon Sinek revealed that he thought everyone expected him to know all the answers. He went on to say that he felt so pressured by these unrealistic and self-made expectations, that if he didn't know an answer he thought it best to pretend that he did.

I smiled with relief when I heard one of the people I most admire in this world admit to feeling this imagined pressure. In my early years as a fitness expert, I too had this unwavering false belief. In both situations, these were unrealistic and self-made expectations. No one had ever said that they expected us to know everything, nor was it possible that we could or would ever know everything—but we both believed it so deeply that these false beliefs became our new truth.

Perfectionists are good at compounding the weight of expectation with fabrication; we are fantastic storytellers when it comes to the stories we tell ourselves.

We magnify our mistakes, minimize our successes, and make up a negative outcome when we have only half the information. A therapist of mine once said that when it comes to dating, women fill in the blanks with fantasy. My thought is that when it comes to the relationship we have with ourselves, we often fill in the blanks with lies and loathing.

Think about the last time you expected something to go perfectly and then it didn't measure up. Could you stop and review the situation, possibly even learn from the experience? Or did you immediately and reflexively begin to pile on more judgment and shame by magnifying your perceived mistakes? An unmet expectation can be a trigger for shame, and nothing compounds this more than putting ourselves under a microscope and magnifying all the thoughts around what we did not do perfectly. When this happens, it can be hard to distinguish where the expectations end and the negative emotions begin. This mindset feeds our doubt demons, moving us into a place of obsessing and checking or paralysis and procrastination. None of which moves us closer to our goals, and all of which pushes us further into our secret internal monologue and away from our relationships and interactions with others.

I first met Lindsay at one of my Perfection Detox workshops in New York City. I remember walking into the yoga studio where I was presenting to see her sitting on the floor journaling. As I entered the room, she looked up and gave me a huge smile and said hello. On first glance, Lindsay looked, well, pretty perfect. She is beautiful, welcoming, and powerful. Lindsay wears a dancer's body, one that is wrapped up in boundless energy. Over the next few hours I came to discover that Lindsay was also wickedly funny, self-deprecating, super smart, and kind.

About an hour into the workshop, I began to talk about the weight of expectations and how they can impact our experiences and limit our joy. As I moved into this conversation, I could see Lindsay's posture begin to sag as she slowly began to retreat inwards. Little did I know that she was carrying the weight of 2,797 miles on her shoulders.

After the workshop was over, I approached Lindsay as I wanted to unpack what I had witnessed before she headed home. We sat cross-legged in a quiet corner of the yoga studio and Lindsay began to open up.

At the time of the workshop, Lindsay had been in New York for two months. She had recently moved to the East Coast after living in Los Angeles for ten years. She moved due to a new job as the game director for a top sports team. This is a job that involves scripting and organizing every aspect (outside of the actual game) of the fans' experience during an event.

As one of the most coveted jobs you can have in this line of work, it came with a lot of pressure and expectations—yet the weight Lindsay was feeling was all self-inflicted. Being a perfectionist, she had expected herself to execute her cross-country transition seamlessly and with unrealistic swiftness. In fact, she had perfectly packaged her moving expectations into a one sheet, containing every detail about how her move was going to go. This also came with pictures from the Internet detailing every move and color-coordinated tabs that separated her personal and professional NYC plans and expectations.

Lindsay had been living in Los Angeles for over ten years; she had mastered her West Coast life. From her local church to her favorite yoga instructor, to her local farmers' market to her deep friendships, Lindsay had designed her life to match both her dreams and her values.

And now here she was after eight weeks in New York City, and she could not understand why her life hadn't already come together perfectly. It had been two months, yet she had yet to feel fully settled in the Big Apple and was still trying to find her footing at her new job. On top of this she was still searching for her favorite yoga class, her new church, and her local farmers' market. And this was the short list. Lindsay was trying to replicate her West Coast life in New York City, and fast.

We began to take a look at her expectations, and Lindsay shared her belief that holding tight to what she knew meant she could control everything. After talking things through with me, I could see Lindsay breathe a little easier, but it would take several more months before she fully found her footing.

During Lindsay's first year in the city she was determined to do the work necessary to help her keep her ambition yet reclaim her joy. She understood that by holding on so tight to keep everything in her reach she was missing out on everything else that was around her. She realized that she wanted to keep the planning so that she could be as prepared as possible, but the big shift was that she learned how to let go of the expectations of what would happen after the plans were in place. As author Joseph Campbell once wisely said: "Sometimes we must let go of the life we have planned, so as to accept the one that is waiting for us."

Lindsay and I recently met for tea and she smiled as she told me of the many magical experiences that appeared in front of her once she let go of how things "should" unfold. These days, instead of a farmers' market she visits a museum, instead of walks on the beach, she strolls through Central Park, and instead of studying with one yoga instructor she has found the flexibility to go to whichever class best fits her busy schedule.

LEAVE YOUR EXPECTATIONS BY THE DOOR

Our expectations often reach deep into our relationships and social interactions, where they have the potential to downgrade positive experiences by taking away our ability to relish in the present. For example, I used to be in the habit of thinking about how to "pay someone back" even before an event was hosted or administered. I never wanted to feel as though I owed anyone anything, so I "helped" preemptively. Never mind looking forward to enjoying the meal or party, or getting ready to mingle—I had to get ready to reciprocate so I could secure my status as the perfect friend.

If you've ever come home from a lovely dinner party at your neighbor's house and immediately started going through the calendar to schedule a reciprocal event as soon as possible, you know what I am talking about. It's not that the hostess was expecting this gesture of reciprocity from you. It's that you felt this is what's expected from a perfect guest.

Expectations can also limit our growth because they place restrictions on what we're willing to ask for in terms of guidance. When I was first began pivoting into speaking and writing, I was hesitant to ask for help as I wondered if my new acquaintances would expect something in return (they didn't), and even worse, if they did, I certainly had nothing worthwhile to offer them in return. This was all in my head, of course, and my efforts to keep track of all the checks and balances, tit for tat, were exhausting and anxiety building. My intentions may have been well meaning, but my fixation on them didn't allow me to enjoy the gift of the present. (Staying in the present is a challenge for the perfectionist and we will return to it throughout the detox.)

Expectations can also get in the way of a good time at just about any time—even when you're on vacation. When I was in the process of writing this book, I would often run ideas by my sister, and when I mentioned this chapter the subject of traveling came up. And this is when I got to hear about the extra baggage I used to place on her.

I could see Jennie take a deep breath and it was obvious that she was deciding whether or not to dive into an experience between us. After I assured her that I wanted to be able to talk about how expectations could impact relationships, she started in on the weight of my expectations around flights, hotels, and evening meals on our travels together. She revealed to me that each time I tried to organize the perfect travel experience for us both, I only added stress instead of joy.

Not once had Jennie said she needed a perfect vacation for it to be a wonderful vacation. While I thought all the planning was a plus, it created a lot of anxiety for her and to be honest, for myself. I constantly worried about the trip not living up to her expectations (none that she had ever shared with me), and in turn Jennie worried how I would react if the trip did not live up to mine. Jennie knew that a great room was often not good enough for me; I needed it to be the perfect room (try that one on when traveling internationally). The evening meals needed to happen in the perfect restaurant, allowing for the most memorable of all evenings to unfold. Yet all Jennie needed for a great vacation was my company and perhaps a good bottle of vino.

All of this resulted in lost hours at the computer as I searched TripAdvisor poring over the hotel and restaurant reviews (often while on vacation). Jennie also reminded me that she would (realistically) expect at least three room changes before asking me, "Can I unpack now?" We laughed as we talked about it, but can you imagine the tension that must have been around every trip, and at the time I was completely oblivious.

In looking back, many of my fondest memories are around the unexpected and spontaneous moments during our trips, including losing my friend Denise for three hours while in Tuscany for my fiftieth birthday. These days, while I still like to book my own travel and hotel, I spend a lot less time obsessing about the perfect trip and focus instead on anticipating more of these unexpected moments and an excellent adventure no matter what. (However, I do still like a nonadjoining room away from the elevator!)

Can you see yourself in any of these scenarios or shades of them? It might take time for you to absorb the idea of expectations and the role they may play in your life, and then a little more for you to be able to observe them. At least now you know what to look for, and where in your life you might need to practice a bit of letting go. By learning to let go of expectations, we make room for goals, which are much healthier for our well-being.

LETTING GO OF HARMFUL EXPECTATIONS, LETTING IN HEALTHY GOALS

Healthy goals energize and motivate us; the fear only creeps in when the expectations we set become impossible to meet due to unrelenting standards.

So how do we know the difference between healthy goal setting and setting unrealistic expectations? Healthy goal setting is driven by intrinsic motivation, giving us room to challenge and stretch ourselves. We set realistic milestones along the way to measure our progress and are able to approach what is in front of us with anticipation, effort, and curiosity. We collaborate and explore, challenge our old way of thinking, and make room for our potential. We reflect often to see how far we have come while embracing the challenge of the work still ahead. Unrealistic expectations are externally motivated by the idea that others expect the impossible from us, they are laced with tension and tinged with fear and keep us looking ahead constantly measuring just how far we still need to go.

An important tool in establishing healthy goals is what's called "SMART" goals. SMART stands for Specific, Measurable, Attainable, Realistic, and Time bound. This simple abbreviation is a very useful benchmark for perfectionists to use and works as a way to ensure that the goals we make set us up for healthy striving and success.

The two key elements in the SMART acronym are *attainable* and *realistic*, neither of which can normally apply to expectations built around perfection. Healthy goals also need to be specific. When we're striving for *perfect* vs. a specific goal, we're working toward a vague, evolving target. This makes it difficult for us to see progress or to acknowledge the skills we already have versus the skills we may still need to sharpen and strengthen.

To help distinguish between a healthy goal and an unrealistic expectation, I want you to ask yourself these key questions:

1. Is this goal *realistic* given my current life situation?

2. Is this goal *attainable* with hard work and effort?
3. Do I have s*pecific* and easy-to-measure milestones in place that I can use to track my progress along the way?

If the answer to all of these is *yes*, it is a good indication that you are stretching yourself in a positive and life-enhancing way. To take Lindsay's experience as an example, the very first question would have given her permission to ease up on herself. A few months down the road perhaps her expectations would be realistic. However, after just two months in a new city to think that she could move across country, find a new place to live, start a new job, and have everything organized and lined up was not doable or even desirable.

When I work with perfectionists, this is the area in which I get some pushback, especially with those in management. They often express fears that if they lower or modify their expectations it will result in lower standards, reduced productivity, and mediocre outcomes. But imagine a corporate culture that is built around the expectations of meeting every goal, every time, and success is measured by perfection. Who is going to step forward with creative and out-of-the-box ideas or with new solutions to old problems? Nobody, as to do so would mean taking a risk, and perfectionism and extreme expectations do not allow room for risk takers.

While I absolutely agree that we need standards and milestones to measure progress and results, unrealistic expectations do not move us closer to these markers. But imagine how striving toward your goals would feel if you removed the expectations and replaced them with a sense of anticipation.

TRYING ANTICIPATION ON FOR SIZE

The Scottish writer Samuel Smiles wrote, "An intense anticipation itself transforms possibility into reality; our desires often being but precursors of the things which we are capable of performing." Anticipation adds the element of excitement and allows room for good things to happen. It also allows room for creativity and exploration and gives us permission to view failures as feedback, pushing out fear. The amount of effort may be the same, but this reframed mindset allows for more ease and joy, which is likely to elevate both morale and productivity. Think of it as an equation:

$$\text{Anticipation} + \text{Action} = \text{Inspired Productivity}$$

Anticipation carries us along the path to our goals. It gives us room to enjoy the journey while at the same time working valiantly to challenge ourselves and reach new heights. Anticipation allows us to stop every now and then to appreciate our efforts, recognize what is working, and also fine tune the parts of the process that may need recalibrating.

Expectations reside on the far side of our goals. They keep us future-focused and are always watching and waiting to make sure everything goes perfectly before releasing their hold on us. On the rare occasions that we do meet our own expectations, our inner critic dusts it off as luck.

For this step, I call on you to become aware of self-defined notions of expectation, obligation, or reciprocity. These can all become mental habits, accumulating over time into an oppressive burden. Ultimately, they choke the pleasure and joy out of essential human interactions.

Of course, I'm not suggesting you become careless or that you start to neglect your obligations. Just think about adjusting *excessive* and *self-imposed* levels of expectation that take you out of the present. Remove the weight of unrealistic expectation and fabrication from your shoulders and focus on creating a stronger bond with your goals and aspirations. You do not need to be perfect to be deserving of a rich, flourishing life that is filled with goals and dreams.

Daily Detox

1. Perfectionists can be great friends. Sometimes, however, we build a list of internal expectations attached to our relationships. Start this part of the detox by paying careful attention to the interactions you have with those to whom you feel you "owe" something—whether it is time, attention, or deed. Is it something that they have explicitly asked of you,

or is it your own inner voice of guilt, doubt, or insecurity speaking? If it is your inner voice, take the time to reflect on the underlying causes for your impulsive need to please. Be a terrific friend, absolutely, but you do not always need to be the one that last did the giving.

2. Notice the expectations that others may place on you. Are they helpful? Are they in alignment with your values and your life? As much as we need to tame our inner critic we also need to turn down the voices of others, especially when they are not in our best interest. If a friend or family member's expectations of you are in conflict with how you want to live your life it may be time for a loving conversation. Gently let them know that while you appreciate them looking out for you, if they cannot support you and your decisions, you would rather they kept their expectations and their opinions to themselves.

3. Manage your own expectations by suspending thoughts about outcomes. For example, when you plan a party, don't try to envision how every guest may assess or judge it. Stay present and fully focused on what will make you enjoy the party and give it 100 percent. Let the attachment to the perfect outcome go. Your guests would rather have you present than perfect.

4. Think about an upcoming event and notice if you have any unrealistic expectations attached to the outcome. Use the SMART system as your measurement scale. Write down what the experience would feel like if you shifted your expectations away from the outcome and onto the actual experience. What would change if the only expectation was to stay present and do your best?

5. Try anticipation on for size. Write down in your journal one thing you anticipate to go well. It could be work related, family related, or simply something you are working toward. Next, write down the action steps needed to close the gap on where you anticipate you want to be and where you are today. Be aware of how you feel as you begin to open a space for inspired action to be created.

Decipher FEAR

For perfectionists, fear is a special, multifaceted adversary. Even though it's just one unpleasant emotion, we find so many ways to spin it in our very own kaleidoscope of catastrophe. There's the fear of being found out, the fear of not doing something perfectly, the fear of saying the wrong thing, the fear of making a mistake, the fear of a less than ideal outcome, the fear of [_____] (insert the one that just came to mind as you were reading this).

Because the scenarios we envision are usually idealized and out of scale, that is, disproportionate to reality, disappointment is as predictable as it is crushing. For the perfectionist, this tendency makes fulfillment or joy—which requires being in the present—especially elusive. The present slips through our fingers as we ponder the mistakes of the past and try to preempt missteps in the future. Over time, we resign ourselves to thinking that nothing will ever be just right and retreat into passivity, as the concrete fear of a future misstep will always override the abstract loss of an opportunity glaring at us in the present.

In this way, fear is a thief, stealing from us memories, connection, and any sort of eagerness or even willingness to try new experiences. And because it can generate generalized anxiety as a byproduct, fear can also be debilitating, humiliating, and demoralizing.

Many people propose that the best way to deal with fear is to get rid of it. But this is a biological impossibility—we were born with the ability to fear, and there are times when we need the reflexive internal response it triggers, times even when our lives depend upon it. We can't deny it, we can't get rid of it, but we can work to understand fear and identify when it's useful or warranted and when it's not. If mastered, this understanding will provide you with one of the most liberating experiences of the detox.

NOTES FROM THE FRONTLINE OF FEAR

Diane (whom you met in Step 1) sent me a note after attending a Perfection Detox workshop: "I seem to operate my life on red alert and I am not sure why I approach everyday tasks as though they are a five-alarm fire. My anxiety and fear of others noticing my anxiety has kept me playing small."

Diane's not the only one; I heard from other women whose deep candor about the constrictions and demands of the perfectionist mindset resonated with me deeply and poignantly. Many shared heart-wrenching reflections on how the quest for perfect had sapped the joy of being in the present moment and opportunity for growth from their lives.

Diane told me later that she was trying to describe just how exhausting it was to want to do everything just right and to capture the consequence of this quest. What had she lost by "living small" I asked her? It was too painful to imagine.

For Diane and other workshop participants, fear had grown so powerful and become such an insurmountable force in their lives that I knew our starting point had to be about bringing fear down to the ground level, or at least into better focus. So I introduced four clarifying thoughts to help push out the fictional version of fear that had taken control of their lives. I think they'll help you, too:

1. Rethink Fear

I like to use the definition of FEAR as "False Expectations Appearing Real." Pulling the curtain back on expectations (as discussed in the previous step) is an important aspect of weakening fear, but the real key to changing our relationship with fear is to understand what is it is, when it holds us back, and when it can actually be a positive force in our lives.

We often forget that many times we feel fear and anxiety because we care, and caring is a wonderful character trait. The more important something is to you, the higher the level of anxiety. The more you stretch and challenge yourself, the more often you will feel afraid. Fear is a sign that you are doing something that matters to you.

People often ask me if I feel afraid when speaking in front of a large group of people. I share that while I no longer feel afraid (false fear) of what people are going to think of me, I do still get nervous. I view my nerves as a sign of caring and a show of respect for my audience. If I wasn't nervous I would be afraid that I had become complacent and careless. So the strategy is to keep the caring, but shift where the care is placed. We move from caring about creating the perfect outcome (too many variables) to caring about how we show up (variable of one).

Another way to shift our perspective on fear is to consider the close relationship between anxiety and excitement and to work to see the former as the latter. Feelings of *excitement* (for what we are doing) and the *anxiety* (of how it may turn out) are both created in the same part of our nervous system called the sympathetic nervous system (SNS). This is the part of our nervous system that moves us into fight or flight and will fire up on all cylinders if we are not in the present. When we are alert and choose carefully the thoughts behind our actions we can shift a fear-based trigger such as "I am anxious about trying something different" over to a positive, simply by changing our inner dialogue: "I am excited and grateful for this new challenge!"

We need to stop viewing fear as a negative. It is in our genetics and was designed to protect us. We reclaim our power when we stop pushing fear away and begin to look at what is underneath our anxious feelings. Was our anxiety triggered by reality, or a really powerful lie created by our doubt demons?

When we accept and explore our anxiety, fear can become one of our greatest teachers. Fear is not the enemy, but as psychologist and meditation teacher Tara Brach tells us, "Fear is a problem when it oversteps its boundaries," and fear loves to step out of bounds whenever it can, especially when left unexamined.

2. Know You're Not Alone

Every perfectionist has been paralyzed by feelings of fear and anxiety, and most of us by the fear that we're not living up to the standards expected of us (self- or other-imposed). A recent poll from the staffing firm Accountemps revealed that 30 percent of people interviewed admitted that making a mistake on the job is their worst fear.

I work with many different people and their stories around perfection. There is one fear that runs through almost everyone's story and that is the debilitating fear of being "found out." We know that feeling like a fraud is one of a perfectionist's most prevalent thoughts and whatever you fear people "finding out" about you will be your perfectionistic Achilles' heel. This one spot will always be open and vulnerable to other people's opinions of you until you face it and reframe it.

The imposter syndrome is not a new concept, but when it comes to perfectionists I see many women carry the extra burden of believing that now they understand what it is, that they should be able to let go of it immediately and of course perfectly.

Recently, I was listening to a good friend of mine speak to this subject during a panel discussion. At her last job, Julie had been a senior vice president at a top technology firm, and for the past three years was a senior VP at a prestigious fashion and cosmetics company. Julie had been sought out for her current role and was thrilled to be at a company that was built for women.

The trouble was that along with her new position, fabulous perks, and salary increase also came her imposter syndrome. When asked how long it took for her to stop feeling like a fraud, her answer was not what you would have expected.

As Julie bravely shared her truth and said the words "two years" I felt the entire room of attendees exhale. All of a sudden hands began to pop up and women throughout the room were asking Julie to share more of her story. Just because we know and understand something does not mean that we can master it overnight.

With Julie's new role came a larger team to manage, a different way of doing things, and an entirely new set of rules, many of which were unspoken. For the first year, she kept feeling as though perhaps they had made a mistake in hiring her, and each time she felt as though she didn't belong she would feed her imposter syndrome and starve her self-esteem.

Julie revealed the deep pain she felt each day that she came to work pretending to be confident, capable, and in control. As much as she knew she had been hired for her strengths and talents and to bring a fresh perspective to the company, she could not shake the feeling that she did not belong. Julie revealed she felt so uncomfortable being called an executive that she often downplayed her role. While everything around her was a symbol of how she had "made it," all Julie could focus on were her gaps and the things that she felt were not going perfectly to plan.

As her feelings of self-doubt deepened they began to suck up her confidence. She often second-guessed herself and rarely asked for help, viewing it as another sign of her being a fraud. Finally as year two came to a close, she felt as though she had managed to figure out what the company wanted, but at her year-end review she was told by her boss that she was not sure if she was going to make it. Two years of trying to duck and dodge mistakes and failures, and her false fears had become a reality.

For the next three months Julie faced her fear head on. It was time to shake up and show up, as what Julie came to realize was that for the past two years she had been trying to do things the way she thought other people wanted. She had put so much weight into other people's ideas, desires, and needs, that she had lost sight of who she was and what she had been hired to do.

Julie decided to do it her way; she dug deep and took the leap and did what she believed was best for the company. Very quickly everything changed. Her colleagues began telling her that she seemed like a completely different person, her boss stopped micromanaging, and she left Julie to create and finish two very important projects.

By being herself and no longer looking to other people for the secret clues, she finally went to her skills, strengths, and experience for the answers, while always asking for help when need be. Julie finally felt that she was more than capable for the job, she had earned her perks, she could manage her team in a way that both they and she flourished, and she went into work each day with a sense of joy and passion.

As a healthy human, it is physiologically and psychologically impossible to not feel afraid. Fear is not the culprit; it is how you respond to the fear that will be the deciding factor. Please remember that you are not alone in your fears and it is not a sign of weakness. We all will struggle with moments of doubt and uncertainty as it is part of the human condition. But we can stand together and remind each other to no longer Forget Everything And Run but Face Everything And Rise.

3. Learn to Spot the Difference: Functional vs. False Fears

Third, understand that your brain does not know the difference between fear that is rational or functional (your toddler is about to step off the curb) or false (your boss can easily see that you don't feel quite ready for the promotion you just received). When it comes to fear, feelings are not facts, but the brain has been known to confuse the two.

When fear and anxiety scramble our mind, the very part of our brain that could help us get out of the confusion, the prefrontal cortex, goes on a mini vacation. As the front part of our brain takes longer to ramp up (it's analyzing the next best move) the oldest part of the brain, the amygdala, sometimes called the reptilian or lizard brain, takes over with gusto. It doesn't need time to think, it just "does." As our brain gets hijacked and moves into fight, flight, or freeze mode, our more logical processing shuts down. This is why fear is so tricky to work with.

To survive and thrive our ancestors had to constantly decide what could hurt them and what would help them. For survival it was more important to focus on the threats versus the treats. The part of your brain that lights up when you feel threatened is the same part of your brain that fires up when you anticipate making a mistake, feel like you are being judged, or think someone will uncover the "real you" behind the façade. Irrational or false fear will remain a source of pain until we change the relationship with the parts of ourselves that we view as flawed.

One of the false fears I had for many years was the idea that when I was out in a social setting I was going to be judged and viewed poorly if I showed up less than perfectly. This first began when I was appearing frequently on television. I was the host of a fitness show that aired regularly on various networks and my brain decided that I needed to be "on and camera ready" at all times.

Eventually, this perception began to filter into every social interaction I had. My faulty fear feelings had become so hard wired that for a while I was also having frequent panic attacks in front of my best friends. To heighten the experience, if a stranger happened to recognize me while I was out and wanted to simply say hello I would go into red alert mode. As they walked over to the table, I would quickly assess what food or alcohol was in front of me and push it over to someone else's place if it wasn't the "perfectly healthy" meal.

Even writing this I feel a tinge of sadness. I missed out on so much and so many great experiences, due to the false fear of having to show up perfectly when out socially. This part of my brain had become so hijacked by my thoughts that it took a long time to untangle.

It was not until many years later when I studied positive psychology and the neuroscience behind the brain's capacity to change based on our repetitive thoughts, did it all click. It is not that my false fear feelings went away overnight, but when I accepted them as a part of who I was they began to lessen their grip.

Can you identify any of your false fears? I encourage you to pay attention next time you feel a wave of anxiety moving in; pause and ask yourself if the fear is warranted or necessary. If it's not, send a message to your brain that you are safe and practice settling down your synapses. I love the idea of saying "hush now" anytime we feel unwarranted anxiety flooding our body. A simple and loving message letting our brain know that we are thankful for it trying to protect us, but at this moment in time it has overstepped its boundaries.

4. Ask Yourself: Is This a Programmed Response?

And lastly, while fear comes off as a present-moment experience, many times it is rather a reaction to a moment that has passed or a preemptive anticipation of a problem in the immediate future. You have made a judgment based on an experience and are therefore expecting trouble. When you are afraid, more often than not you have either slipped into the past, or are worrying about the future.

One of the trickiest things about real fear and false fear is that they both appear at the snap of a thought. This is frustrating and can feel distressing at times. For perfectionists the false fear triggers are more often than not personalized. Our brain has turned on itself and become programmed to view our mistakes and flaws as something to feel ashamed of and be afraid of. As we know the more our brain repeats something the stronger the programming becomes, but just because it is programmed does not make it real.

We begin to deprogram our faulty fear thinking by learning to look at our thoughts, versus looking at the world through our thoughts. An exercise that has helped me create distance between who I am and what I think, is being impeccable with my words, especially the words I use with myself. My language used to sound like "I'm afraid of not showing up perfectly," and I learned to rephrase that statement to, "I am having a feeling about not showing up perfectly." This allows me to create a space between the thought I am thinking and the life I am living. I am able to stop personalizing the sensation and go underneath the feeling to find out what the real fear trigger is. It is the difference between *having* a thought and *being* the thought, the difference between making a mistake and thinking we are the mistake.

The way to filter out the false fear is to remain as present as possible especially when a false fear kicks in. That last sentence is almost impossible to do, however the act of being aware and catching yourself each time you notice the soul-sucking emotion of fear washing over you is one step closer to detoxing from the anxious thoughts that are rooted in lies.

Working with fear takes time. It also takes acceptance, awareness, and a ton of self-appreciation for showing up and doing the work. The fact you are on this journey is already putting your false fears on alert. They know you're beginning to figure out the games they play, and it is only a matter of time before you give them a time-out (for good). Until that moment there are probably going to be times that you will need to show up and act "as if" until your brain catches up. There is nothing wrong in doing the work afraid.

THE KEY TO MAKING PEACE: YOUR PRESENCE

When a perfectionist feels fear she sees it as more proof that she is not handling her life perfectly. Viewed as another flaw, fear is pushed away into the background, which gives it more negative power. Avoidance of anything only adds more fuel to the situation. If we are to reach a truce with our fears or develop a useful degree of understanding and compassion, we have to show up to the peace talks.

When helping a patient overcome a fear or a phobia, many therapists recommend exposure therapy. For perfectionists, this means exposure to what we fear and fight against most: our particular, specific fears.

This might mean creating scenarios that mimic failure. Pavel Somov, a psychologist who specializes in perfectionism, has suggested fascinating exercises for combating fear of mistakes and anxiety associated with potential lack of approval. For example, he offers this fear-management opportunity: when you are at a red light which turns green, take a few moments before letting go of the brake. You'll hear a lot of honking, and if your windows are open, some cursing and maybe even name calling. But the world will not end; and once you press the gas pedal, the haters won't bother giving you another thought. Or, Somov suggests, deliberately mispronounce a word, make a self-deprecating joke, or be a nuisance to others. You'll see that initial discomfort doesn't produce any lasting outcomes so your fear of it is both exaggerated and beatable.

I think such steps are bold and creative, but in practice, I've found that few people will want to make a mistake deliberately as an exercise. Still: If you are feeling adventurous or curious, I encourage you to try these experiments.

Perfectionists often feel a wide disconnect between their fears of the future and the future that they desire. We don't understand why we just can't seem to get over it and get on with it. Lolly Daskal, author of *The Leadership Gap*, tells us "what you don't own owns you!" and this is especially true when it comes to our fears. Avoidance is like Miracle-Gro for your doubt demons. But when we examine our anxiety through the lens of compassion, fear will no longer be our foe.

These detox steps helped Diane and other participants in my program, and I hope they will help you, too. Learning to manage anxiety about the future allows us eventually to release our inner judgment and shift our focus onto something more rewarding than trying to anticipate what can possibly go wrong.

Daily Detox

❖ The physical symptoms of fear may be individualized, but they are very real. When you are afraid or anxious, your stomach constricts, your chest tightens, your heart beats faster, and your face flushes. Pay attention and acknowledge your individual symptoms of fear, but shift your focus to the present. If you are sitting, stand up. If you are standing, walk. Just move. Bring attention to your breathing, try to slow it down, and lengthen the exhale. Think of anxiety that arouses from fear as excitement without the oxygen—simply by adding the breath you can downgrade anxiety into excitement. Breathe in for four counts and out for eight. Repeat for a minute. As you breathe in, say to yourself "Be here now," and as you exhale say "This too shall pass."

❖ Use the SOAR-Q (Stop, Observe, Adjust, Reflect, Question) exercise to uncover the trigger behind your fear feeling and reframe your thoughts in relation to the fear. I've used this exercise a great deal in my own life. If I feel fear before I go onto a large stage to speak, I use this process to prevent falling into my negativity bias. Here's how my SOAR-Q would look:

1. I **Stop** and notice the feelings of anxiety that stem from me telling myself I need to deliver the perfect speech.

2. I **Observe** how this makes me feel and decide if I need to make changes.

3. I **Adjust** my self-talk to say: "It does not need to be perfect to make a difference; if I change or help one person in the audience of eight hundred, it has been a good day."

4. I **Reflect** upon my focus on trying to give the perfect speech and reframe it. Instead of trying to get a five-star evaluation, I aim to provide the audience with a five-star experience. In other words, I think more about helping someone rather than having my effort be consciously validated by them.

5. I then ask myself a **Question**: what action step can I take to help cement the reframed mindset? In this case, I find that concrete physical moves help quell the excess adrenaline and anxiety. Jumping in place works, heel lifts in place if you are tight on time and space, or my favorite, a quick power walk. You pick what feels right to you. It may be moving your body or it may be simply moving your breath.

Whose Voice Is in Your Head?

CHRONIC NEGATIVE SELF-TALK DOES NOT EXIST IN A VACUUM. IT HAS ORIGINS FIRMLY planted in the past, and with future-plaguing consequences. If you are to regain a strong foothold in the present—the only place we're meant to be!—you must investigate these origins and their relationship to some of your most limiting self-perceptions.

Growing up, the phrases that had a disproportionate impact on my perception of myself, and in turn the course of my life, were "Your father is a drunk," "You look like a slut," and "You could stand to lose a couple of pounds." These toxic words and the emotions they evoked stayed with me for decades, and were repeated in my head so often and for so long that at some point I lost the ability to hear them in the original voice they were spoken—eventually, they were delivered in my own voice.

I look like a slut, I said to myself when a gentleman's glance lingered a second too long on my face. I am so unfit, I reflected when the skinny jeans felt a little tight. The voices came up for me whenever I felt as though I could not control an outcome, and they sounded so much like my own that I believed that they were.

It took seven years of therapy for me to finally hear these words in the original voices of people long gone. I remember the shock of identifying them. I even remember the moment. I was in New York City, getting ready to go out to a special event. I looked at the mirror and heard "you look like a slut" coming out of nowhere. And I realized the voice belonged to my now very elderly, if living, dance teacher. And the words had nothing to do with who I was, not then and not when the words were originally uttered. They were just careless expressions of her opinion, and an incorrect one at that.

In many cases, dismantling these loaded messages will lead to the discovery of an unstable foundation—one that's not as unyielding as you believe it to be. Simply by confronting this shaky basis of our beliefs, we can diffuse the shame and disappointment it's been reinforcing for so many years.

THE STORIES THAT SHAPE US

It's easy to think that only *your* mother, father, or other influential person in your early life delivered a formative, possibly painful message. It's easy because, let's face it, the topic isn't likely to come up in casual dinner conversation. But let me tell you this: you are far from alone if this was part of your experience. I realized this when I provided a space where people could discover, explore, and share their own stories—and when I first broke the ice with my own story.

During my first 21-Day Perfection Detox Program one of the participants, Connie, talked of her experience that on the surface seemed different in substance from mine, but was so close in terms of its childhood origins.

Connie had gone to a strict Catholic school, where a test score of 98 was not enough. If you could get 98 on a test, the nuns told her, why not 100? This rigid perspective was reinforced by Connie's father, a military sergeant who expected his kids to be as perfect as he was in all their endeavors. An attentive father, he was watching the kids to make sure they were living up to their potential, in the process making Connie extremely self-conscious and fearful of a misstep. "If I slipped up," she recalled, "my fear of making a wrong decision would haunt me for days."

She realized that throughout her life she had passed on opportunities just to avoid the dread of a possible mistake. Her father may have meant well when he wanted

Connie to be the best that she could be, but his unyielding vigilance ended up doing just the opposite—preventing her from reaching her potential since she was constantly holding back, afraid of doing anything less than perfectly. "I realize now that life is too short and that I am the one who has missed out," Connie concluded. The detox helped her to live and breathe in the moment by letting go of the voices from the past—especially her father's. The best news is that Connie is now paying her own work forward by mentoring young girls ages eight to eleven in a running club.

Stories like Connie's are all around us, some lying dormant, some stashed as secrets where they can breed shame. But it's time for them to come out in this detox. As you've been reading this chapter, perhaps you've been thinking about the words and phrases that were spoken to you years ago, the ones that still echo through your head. Can you hear the messages that were delivered? Can you hear whose voice is speaking? Can you remember how old you were? The messages that define us are often delivered to us in our early years, so be patient and don't worry if nothing appears right away. Tread lightly and know that you can revisit your past at any time to complete this step.

THE SEEDS OF SELF-ESTEEM

We are born whole and live that way until the day someone rejects or reshapes us. The first time we hear a disapproving comment from a person whom we admire or from whom we are craving approval is the day that our whole self starts to splinter and separate. As the first wave of disappointment and shame washes over us, our self-esteem begins to slowly wash away.

As children, we are especially vulnerable, absorbent beings; our sense of self is *dependent* on others. We lack the experience that would allow us to question someone else's opinion of us, and the messages that flow in are therefore likely to be the ones that help form our self-esteem or self-worth.

Research has shown that self-esteem begins to develop around the age of five. Early childhood educator Ellen Booth Church tells us that children around the ages of five to six are already wondering if they will be liked when they start school.

Our self-esteem goes on to be strengthened or weakened in our teenage years, when a combination of external influences, including our parents, role models such as coaches and teachers, and our friends and peers can build us up or break us down.

If a coach or role model tells you during these formative years that you are too lazy, too stupid, too weak, too fat, too sensitive, you eat too much, don't try hard enough, and so on, it's incredibly hard not to believe them.

Your sense of self-worth will continue to ebb and flow throughout your life, but it's these early seeds that can be the trickiest to unearth and untangle, especially because they are often associated with people you loved and admired. We are more prone to personalize and internalize the criticisms made by people important to us (or about people important to us, in my case), and to let these chip away at our self-esteem. In someone with perfectionistic tendencies, an extreme need to prove that we belong, that we are deserving, and that we are worthy can set in. When you have to work so hard to validate your presence, you're permanently taken out of the present.

As we slowly remove the limiting beliefs from our past, we replace them with building blocks that allow us to flourish and thrive in the present. These blocks are created by focusing on and strengthening the best parts of ourselves, which in turn creates a strong and healthy self-esteem. Nathaniel Branden, who was a leader in this field of work, defined self-esteem as trusting our own mind and knowing that we are worthy of happiness.

A healthy self-esteem is one of the cornerstones to being able to reclaim a life of joy and is built on the pillars of self-acceptance, self-responsibility, self-assertiveness, living consciously, in integrity, and with purpose. When placed together they create an unshakable barrier between the voices of our past and the life we are creating today.

For a while self-esteem was getting a ton of negative press. Associated with ego and bravado, people questioned whether high self-esteem was a positive character trait.

But when we talk about self-esteem in relation to having a sense of self-efficacy and self-respect, self-esteem gives us the capacity to show up fully and help others rise too, just as Connie is doing with the girls from her running club. It is a fundamental part of ourselves that we need to cultivate and tend to as we detox from perfection.

START TO PAY ATTENTION TO YOUR BUCKET FILLERS

In 2006, Carol McCloud published *Have You Filled a Bucket Today?*, a small yet profound book. Its message is both simple and powerful: we all have a bucket and at every moment it is either being filled or emptied by the things people say or do to us. When it is full we feel great and when it is empty we feel miserable.

Reflect back and ask yourself, "Who emptied my bucket?" Those are the voices we want to let go of. Now ask yourself, "Who filled my bucket?" Those are the voices we need to pay more attention to. Anytime we visit our past (unless it is with a licensed therapist) we tread lightly and cautiously. We are not mining for deep wounds here, but we are looking for experiences that we may have brushed off for many years as "nothing."

Many of my negative thoughts came in the voices of people I had admired as I was growing up. "You are not smart enough" and "You look like a slut" belonged to various teachers that I trusted; "You are too fat" was the voice of the choreographer I worshiped. A decade later as my fitness career was beginning to take off, and since my self-esteem was already on shaky ground, these opinions fueled my own voice that said, "You need to be a perfect fit to fit into fitness" . . . and so the downward spiral of toxic thoughts continued.

YOU DON'T HAVE TO GO INTO THE PAIN CAVE

Any time we look back and remember something that is not a positive there is a risk that we will move into rumination. This is not what I am asking you to do in this step. I simply want you to become more aware of the effects that these voices may have had on you, and will continue to do so if left to their own devices.

The types of situations I am asking you to recall are moments that easily come to mind. Perhaps you can remember a time when one of your role models carelessly tossed a criticism your way. Because you respected them and craved their approval, you not only felt the criticism but also grabbed it and ran with it. Or perhaps a coach you admired broke you down but forgot to build you back up. Maybe some fickle friends suddenly decided you were no longer a part of their clique for some reason. These voices can be subtle and yet so toxic when it comes to our thought loops. This step is going to help dial down the negative voices into a whisper and then flush them out with forgiveness.

As you look back to the people in your past who may have carelessly said something to you that made you feel "less than" I want you to balance that by leaning into the people of your past who celebrated and supported you. Try to also recall a role model worthy of your admiration, someone who told you that you could do anything with effort, praised your hard work, and reminded you that you deserved to have the very best out of life. These are the voices that we want to turn up and tune into. Believe them to be true and meet yourself there.

Daily Detox

1. Who do the negative voices in your head belong to? If you are not sure, go back to your role models around the ages of six to sixteen. My guess is there is someone during that period whom you looked up to, who told you in some way or another that you were either too much or not enough. Skim the surface of your memories and see if anything pops up. Using the wellness scale; ask yourself which voices filled your bucket by adding joy to your life and which voices sucked the joy out of you by emptying your bucket?

2. Work on restructuring your response to the voices in your head. Instead of listening to them, believing them, and leaping to the same reflexive action, become a bit insubordinate—reject the notion and reframe it. In my case, I shifted "You look like a slut" to "You look like someone who is meant to shine"—and help others do the same. Reflect, reframe, and reboot.

3. This last step is one that you complete now or can come back to further into the detox; either option will work for the detox process. I say this because it involves forgiveness, which has to be heartfelt and one that you feel ready for. However, I do encourage you to complete this step before the end of the detox, as when we forgive others for the hurt they have caused, it opens up more room in our head and heart for the good stuff to flow in. Forgiveness is not forgetting, or even letting people off the hook if they hurt you with

their words. But it is unhooking yourself from the negative voices of your past so that they no longer can affect your positive future. The flip side of forgiveness is responsibility, and self-responsibility is one of the pillars of self-esteem.

Why is it important to forgive? Because, to paraphrase author Louise Hay, most people are doing the best they can given what they know and understand. If they knew more and were aware of more, they would do things differently. Just as my father did the best that he could with what he knew, so did the people whose voices you still hear today. It's important to make peace, more so for your own recovery than anyone else's.

It wasn't until I finally made peace with the fact my father had been an alcoholic that the voice about my father being a drunk eventually became a whisper. As I came to understand that he had done the best that he could with the life tools that he had been given, I began to be able to forgive him. He modeled his parents, who had also been heavy drinkers, and he had wanted nothing more than his father's approval. Being open to knowing his full story allowed me to discover that my aunt, who lived in Australia and to whom I was not close, had also passed away at a young age from health issues related to alcohol.

This horrible disease had robbed my father of so much, including a healthy relationship with me, that I decided to make peace with that part of my past so it would no longer rob me of a powerful present. It's true that there isn't always a disease to consider when we think back to the voices of the people who hurt us, but there is always a bigger picture to someone else's story, one which we may not understand. This is about releasing the negative voices so that it is you, and not the people of your past, who will be writing your best-self story in the future.

Write a short letter to the person in your past whose voice is the loudest today. This letter is not going to be sent, but it does need to be sincere. You will tear it up as soon as it is written destroying both the letter and symbolically the part of your past that was destroying you. This is all about your experience. In the letter describe the moment when the person wronged you with their words. Be sure to include the emotions that you were feeling during that time. Then read your letter with a feeling of forgiveness, knowing that this person was probably thinking they were helping you. As you tear up the letter and throw it away, say to yourself, "I release, I am enough, I am complete."

Remember that forgiveness is a gift to yourself, not to the person or events that create pain in your past. If the voice that is resounding most loudly in your head is your own, feel free to write this letter to yourself.

STEP 6

Work with Your Imperfections Instead of Pushing Them Away

ACCEPTANCE AND COMPASSION, PARTICULARLY TOWARD THE SELF, ARE ESSENTIAL GOALS OF the Perfection Detox. However, both can be a great challenge because they involve, at least at the beginning, going against your impulse to try to change the imperfect to perfect, no matter what the cost. Before we can fully detox from the parts of perfection that do not serve us, we need to disable, or at least weaken, this impulse by deploying the power of acceptance. We need to fully accept who we are today, including our real and perceived flaws.

We don't get to pick and choose the parts of ourselves we want to keep and the parts we want to ignore. Acceptance is like a cleanser for the palate of the soul. And just as you need to cleanse your palate before you are introduced to a whole new taste, you need to give your soul a clean slate before we move to the next phase of reclaiming joy. You need to be aware and prepared, but you don't need to be perfect to improve your attitude or circumstances. You just need a fresh outlook. As psychologist Carl Rogers said, "when I accept myself just as I am, then I can change."

And this is, after all, what I hope you create with this detox: a positive, cleansing change, one that liberates you from the restrictive chains of perfectionism, strips away its toxic effects, and lets you fall in love again—or maybe for the first time—with your one precious self. Because that's certainly what you deserve. In the absence of acceptance, love struggles to survive, while an internal war thrives. Deepak Chopra wrote that we must accept *what* happens to us with open arms or else we risk constant clashing in our minds. This is true of accepting *who* we are, too. When we accept ourselves, we dissolve the internal conflict and struggle between the person we are and the person we think we should be.

In this step, I want you to make progress on the path to self-acceptance. The journey starts with some awareness and will require a stop to fill up on self-compassion, and you likely won't get all the way there in one straight shot, but the goal is to get you moving in the right direction.

FIRST COMES AWARENESS

For perfectionists, acceptance begins with awareness of what we define as success. All too often, we saddle ourselves with a wildly unrealistic, unattainable definition of what it would it mean to have finally achieved the holy grail of success with a capital S or a capital P. We need to be perfect moms, perfect wives and partners, perfect friends, the perfect employee—*Hello, who are we fooling when we think all these are possible and possible at the same time?*

I've come to call this strictly defined, structured definition of success the "faux full package." Why faux? Because it's not based on reality, but instead on an unreachable ideal. This ideal is dangerous since it is when we perpetually try and fail to live up to it that we create an insurmountable road block between ourselves and self-acceptance. To open the roadway, we have to start by redefining what the full package means to us. Only then can we let compassion in, which operates like a bridge and can get us all the way across to the ultimate goal of acceptance.

I was once talking with the father of a young woman struggling with the perfectionist mindset. When I asked him why she was struggling so much, he said, "Because she feels as though she needs to be the 'full package' to be successful." I instantly understood what he meant because as a former professional dancer, fitness expert, and television personality, I too suffered under the yoke of having to be a "full package" or rather what I *thought* being a full package entailed. In my eyes being the full package meant that I had to be a size 2 and electrifying on screen, and that I had to perpetually emanate health, vitality, and joy (which I could, mind you, no longer feel at most times). In other words, I had to be the version of myself that you would see in a two-minute clip on the *Today* show or frozen in time on a Times Square billboard, not the one you would run into in real life.

It took years of therapy for me to realize that I had been envisioning the "full package" incorrectly all along. I thought the full package meant I had to be perfect on the inside and out at all times. I thought to succeed professionally I had to love my workouts all the time (I didn't; in fact, they were a huge effort for me), eat a clean diet all the time (which bored me to tears and reminded me of the struggles I had with food in my twenties), and stay away from alcohol all the time (anyone who knows me can attest to my affection for a glass or two of Chardonnay). Forcing myself to follow these rules all the time made me miserable.

I eventually arrived at the conclusion that while I was striving for the full package, I was settling for half a package and ultimately isolating myself further into my perfectionistic cocoon. By constantly going full throttle and presenting my perfect façade to the outside world, I was only moving myself further away from being someone that people could relate to. This wasn't the full package, it was only half the package, if that. For the full package to emerge we need contrast. We need good days and not-so-good days, the ebbs and flows and hits and misses; we need our highlight reel and our backstory. Realizing that a perfect package and a full package weren't the same thing and that what I was envisioning was really a "faux package" was a profound revelation for me. That awareness allowed new sprouts of self-acceptance to begin to form.

The author and speaker Jenny Blake has a super successful podcast and her work has been recommended by the likes of Seth Godin and featured on CNBC—in other words she is the full package. Yet when the lights went off, the microphone was put away, and the book signings ended, there was a side of her that felt anything but, particularly when it came to her budding romantic relationship.

We are good friends and often talk about our struggles with perfection. Jenny's need for perfection was rooted in the idea that if she was not perfect, how would she be able to maintain a relationship? If she gained weight or didn't wear make-up, for example (even though she knew deep down these concerns were about the superficial things in life), would he stick around? On deeper exploration the bigger lie that had been hiding in the shadows was, "If I am not perfect, I am not lovable, and so then who am I to be worthy of a fulfilling and long-lasting relationship?" Although Jenny had reached a state of acceptance, self-trust, and faith in the unknown when it came to running her business, she realized that her romantic life had been starved of these same crucial ingredients.

What Jenny came to see was that (1) this was no way to live, and (2) to grow and to lean into this relationship would require making friends with her fears and imperfections. Jenny now sees the many parallels between our work life and our personal life. She believes that our imperfections, our fears, and our uncertainties, the very parts of our selves that we keep hidden from view, can be our super-strengths that will enable us to step into our full potential.

We can have the perfection calculator on at all times, tallying our every imperfection and flaw, but what if everything we thought was making us "less than" added up to the sum of a magnificent human being?

An important part of this realization involved redefining what being the full package meant to me. As it turns out, it didn't mean that I had to be perfect and love everything 24/7; in fact, in most cases I could arrive at the same result simply by doing my best and accepting the outcome no matter what. Sometimes that happened to be perfect and sometimes, well not so much. By easing up on the throttle this way, I settled down and let myself go with the ups and downs of life. Wouldn't you know—this adjustment softened my shell and allowed people to see me as someone they could relate to. It turns out that imperfect is easier to relate to than perfect. This shift in perspective changed my relationships with clients and opened opportunities for my inner and financial growth.

Now I want to ask you—can you see ways that you could redefine what it means to you to be a full package? Is your full package really a faux one? Gaining some perspective here can, as I shared with the concerned dad, relieve some of the pressure we place upon ourselves, and let us start making progress along the path to self-acceptance. But remember: we can't get all the way there without reinforcing or building the bridge of self-compassion.

LETTING COMPASSION IN

Kristin Neff, Ph.D., associate professor at the University of Texas and author of the book *Self-Compassion,* defines self-compassion as having three core components: self-kindness, mindfulness, and a recognition of our common humanity. When we can be our own advocate and work from a place of kindness, when we can remember that our power lies in the present moment, and when we realize we are more alike in our struggles than we are different, our lives begin to sweeten. We learn how to offer ourselves the hugs and approval that we have been longing for from others.

Imagine how your world will look when you replace self-judgment with self-compassion. When the negative self-talk is replaced with loving words that encourage you to work hard and thrive. A quick check-in that you can use anytime and anywhere is to imagine you have a thought bubble attached to your head. In this bubble pops up all the thoughts you have about yourself for everyone else to see. Think about the last string of thoughts you had. Would you feel comfortable saying them to anyone else? Would you feel comfortable with others seeing how you talk to yourself?

Ralph Waldo Emerson once wrote, "To be yourself in a world that is constantly trying to make you something else is the greatest accomplishment." This is so true and hard enough when we are trying to live up to everyone else's standards, let alone when we add the pressure of our own unrealistic markers of success. As you direct more compassion your own way, acknowledge this act in and of itself as an accomplishment. And don't hold back—be rebelliously, unabashedly compassionate; you've got some lost time to make up for. The greater the degree of compassion you direct your own way, the further along you will put yourself on the path to acceptance.

SELF-ACCEPTANCE: THE ULTIMATE PEACE PACT
BETWEEN YOU AND YOURSELF

Nathaniel Branden, who as I mentioned was a psychotherapist and best-selling author on self-esteem, characterized self-acceptance as a "refusal to be in an adversarial relationship with myself." This means that instead of engaging in a constant war with the parts of ourselves we view as flawed, we begin to recognize that it is the sum of all our parts—the good, the bad, and the in between—that creates our beautiful, unique being.

Acceptance is one of the key ingredients to creating a happier life, however it is also one of the hardest practices to establish as a habit. In a recent survey by the charity Action for Happiness, five thousand people were asked about ten happiness habits and how often they "practiced" them. Practicing kindness through giving was the top habit, while acceptance, which was ranked through answers to the question "How often are you kind to yourself and think you're fine as you are?" came in last with a score of 5.6 out of 10. Of the ten happiness habits listed in the survey, cultivating the habit of self-acceptance was found to be the strongest predicator to our happiness, but the weakest link in the chain forming emotional wellness.

Self-acceptance is a contract we make with ourselves to never betray our own authentic self for who we think the world wants us to be. Think of the many betrayals we make every day as we compromise our happiness to meet the unrealistic and often false expectations that can be found all around us. Imagine how our heart must shrink a little every time we look in the mirror and our eyes lock onto the areas we despise, and once again we silently chastise ourselves for showing up imperfectly.

The reality is that we are neither perfect nor imperfect. We are on a journey to be better, but perfection is not and should not be the destination. There will be moments when everything aligns—your goals, your hard work, the timing—and you hit it out of the park, and there will be moments when we try our best, do the work, but the timing is just not in our favor and the project, the relationship, or the whatever fizzles. All of this is called life. When we can accept that some of the variables can't be predetermined rather than ruthlessly judge outcomes, when we can learn as oppose to blame, and when we take full responsibility and accept where we are today, the weight of perfectionism will get lighter.

Self-acceptance allows us to move into flow (you'll read more about flow in Step 19) as it removes the constant chatter of negativity and allows us to be in the present without a running commentary and judgment. Think about all the moments we lose when we are pushing against what is. Acceptance is another tool that moves us closer to our power zone of the present moment. It is accepting who we are today and the idea that "I am enough" combined with the effort and action to keep us moving toward our goals, "I am enough *and* there is still work I want to do."

Operating from a place of self-acceptance also allows you to take more risks and show up bright, bold, and ready to create opportunities or take them when they're presented. Research from the field of positive psychology shows that people with more self-acceptance and self-compassion have more resilience, optimism, curiosity, and a higher level of life satisfaction. You soar to new heights because you are no longer wasting precious energy and mental resources battling with your own life.

For many perfectionists, embracing all that you are also means learning how to acknowledge and appreciate your goodness: your strengths, your passions, your sensuality, your work ethic, your joy, your pride, your accomplishments, your awe, and your wonder. Just like we perfectionists are good at magnifying or making up stories to support our perfectionistic tendencies, we are also masters at minimizing the good. "I was lucky," she tells her co-workers when she gets the promotion she worked so hard for; "Oh, you like this top—it was on sale at Target last week," we mutter when someone compliments our clothes; "It was nothing," you say as you brush aside the praise showered on you for helping the team last minute and saving the deal. When someone compliments a perfectionist, the reflexive action is to either minimize it and/or then add a clarifier. This is our inner critic trying to protect us. "Don't get a big ego," she will whisper. "Say something negative about yourself before they do," she will say. Think about the last time someone paid you a compliment. Were you able to simply say, "thank you," or did you find yourself adding something after those two little words to downplay your light?

To keep moving forward and upward we need to balance honoring our strengths with recognizing the areas we still want to work on and strengthen. I once watched an interview with the legendary Quincy Jones, who was talking about the passing of Whitney Houston. In it, he discussed the pain of singers who always were striving to hit the high note with the idea that the perfect note was the only note. He said problems arose when artists let the praise go to their heads and the critics get to their hearts. This can be said of self-acceptance. Don't let your strengths go to your head and don't let doubt get to your heart. It is a balance, and each day will be a different in where the weight is placed, but it is no longer weighing you down.

Your inner critic might try to run interference on your efforts to achieve self-acceptance and find balance in all-or-nothing equations. She's fantastic at negating your strengths and downgrading your success. She panics at the thought of you stepping out of the fear zone and into the light. She wants to protect you from the risk of failure or of being found out, but it is only when we have the courage to show up fully and without apology that the magic moments will unfold.

Just like forgiveness does not mean condoning, acceptance does not always mean completely liking what you see. But it does allow us to objectively view the parts of ourselves that still may need strengthening and improving. Instead of punishing ourselves for the areas of our lives that are not perfect, we can use the lens of self-acceptance to see that our potential has not yet been met. When we focus positively on this potential, we make room for appreciation and enthusiasm and open the door to feelings of excitement about continuing to work toward our goals.

ACCEPTANCE, NOT ACQUIESCENCE

Acceptance is not about ignoring our weaknesses, but instead requires a shift in how we react to our imperfections and mistakes. Rather than beat ourselves up, we accept that as human beings we will have character faults and flaws. Then we get to look them head on and decide if we can live with our rough edges, or if we want to do some work to narrow the gap between our today and our potential. This is where the serenity prayer can be a wonderful gut check, "God, grant me the serenity to accept the things I cannot change, the courage to change the things I can and the wisdom to know the difference." (Feel free to replace "God" with whatever suits your personal preference.)

Life is here to teach us, and everything we need to learn will be put in our path, including our struggles with perfectionism. When I was first diagnosed over twenty years ago with cancer, and during the two weeks when I was waiting to see what type of cancer it was, I remember thinking one thing, "I want to be around long enough to love as I know I can love." I used to think that this was the act of loving someone else. But I came to realize it was the act of learning to love myself. It took me another fifteen years to get there, but it was worth the journey.

Daily Detox

1. Make a list of what you perceive are your top three Imperfections. (Note that if procrastination happens to be on your list, we will be taking a much closer look at this topic in Step 12.) When making this list also consider the impact you have on those around you. If you are always late, that is something you would want to work on and change, as it is probably impacting your relationship with others in a negative way. However, if you occasionally run a couple of minutes late due to unforeseen circumstances and you beat yourself up for hours after the fact, then it is something to target in the detox. Just recently at a Perfection Detox workshop, a participant named Joanna shared with me that she almost didn't attend. Joanna wanted to finish her graduate work before leaving for the event and found herself running five minutes late. She came into the room quietly and cautiously only a few minutes after I had begun, with no negative impact to the workshop. At the end of the event Joanna told me that the thought of being even a few minutes late was enough for her to consider not coming at all. I am so glad she changed her mind, as her feedback (or feed forward) to the workshop was so insightful that it helped me improve the content of the workshop I presented the following month. Ideally, the items on your list will be specific and ones that you can apply action to. For example: "I need to be perfect at work" is a sweeping statement that only causes more anxiety. However, writing down, "I never know all the answers at the management meetings and to be the perfect manager I believe I should know all the answers" is something we can work with. This is a crucial step to your detox as it will allow you to start the transition from needing to appear perfect to working toward being your best.

2. Look at the list of your top three imperfections and reflect if any of these have a negative impact on your own life. For many perfectionists we see our imperfections through our appearance, the one we see in the mirror and the one that we show to the world. When we really dial it down and look at the negative impact, the disruption is all in our

mind. And while these thoughts do limit our joy and our ability to be present on a daily basis they are not nearly as problematic as we think.

Make peace with and accept your "imperfections" by exploring the possibility that they can be—and often are—harmless. In fact, these imperfections may be the gateway to your greatness. You will find that most of what you see as "imperfections" are probably natural features of being human. For example, one "imperfection" on my list would have been "When I am on stage, I should know every answer to be the perfect presenter." Looking back, I can now see that I was setting myself up to strive for impossible standards, i.e., guaranteed failure. No one person knows everything (except for maybe the late Stephen Hawking, but even he acknowledged one could only have as much as a theory on everything). When I reframed that perceived imperfection to always showing up prepared, but letting go of the need to know everything, my presentation skills (and evaluations) soared. I was seen as more approachable, more engaged, and funnier. When it comes to character strengths (which we will talk about in Step 11), one of mine is humor. I was so concerned at the thought of being "found out" it never allowed me to be in the moment and react to funny moments. After I stopped obsessing and was able to be present, I would naturally find spontaneous interactions with the audience that brought laughter and ease into the room. When I was no longer being mentally three steps ahead waiting for myself to trip up, the audience was able to feel as though they were in conversation with me versus being talked to.

Alongside each perceived imperfection write a positive reframe on how you can move your imperfection from a liability over to an asset.

3. Choose one of your perceived imperfections. Imagine it is now your best friend who is struggling with this thought. Write a short letter to your friend telling her what you see. Through the lens of acceptance and compassion, what would you tell her? How would you encourage her to shift her perspective to one that is more nurturing? What strengths would you remind her of and what changes would you suggest she make to be kinder to herself? Once you have completed the letter, slowly read it back to yourself. Can you begin to see yourself and accept yourself for just how incredible you already are?

STEP 7

Lifting the Shame Layer

SHAME IS THE LAST LAYER THAT KEEPS US FROM RECLAIMING AND REVEALING OUR TRUE selves. For most of us, this layer was laid down the first time someone made us feel that we were "less than perfect"—and it typically takes going back to this moment to start to strip the shame away.

If even the thought of shame makes you feel a little squeamish, you're not alone. It's natural to recoil from shame, even more so for perfectionists, who see this powerful and often painful emotion as the poster child for imperfection. But as with other emotions, rejection only gives it greater strength. For me, and for other perfectionists, understanding, processing, and recognizing the triggers that drop us into a shame spiral was essential to recovery. This will no doubt be true for you, too.

We may not be able to burn up all the shame in this one step, but gaining an understanding of what it is and exploring why we have shame will help release much of the toxicity that it carries. We must come to the table with the emotions and parts of ourselves that we're not comfortable with. When these remain unaddressed, we let stand the silent barrier that exists between us and our full potential. It's time to knock it down.

FIFTY SHADES OF SHAME

Shame is part of a group of emotions called self-conscious emotions. Guilt, embarrassment, and pride are also in this category. Self-conscious emotions can elicit varying degrees of discomfort. From the slight embarrassment that happens when you burp in an elevator in front of strangers, or a slightly deeper embarrassment when you fart ("windy pooh" as my mother used to call them) in a yoga class (yep, that has happened to me too!) to the more deeply rooted shame that can leave us feeling isolated and separate from those around us. This last shade of shame is much harder to shake off.

In *The Science of Shame and Its Treatment*, Gerald Loren Fishkin writes, "Shame is mysterious and elusive by nature. Shame can cause a wide range of behaviors, but escapes detection or understanding because we cannot see or touch or measure it. We can only experience it." He goes on to say, "the experience of shame is a state of being." In other words it is feeling ashamed for who we are.

Shame, when left unresolved over time, will affect us in two ways. We either collapse into the shame, feeling broken and questioning our worth, or we will rise above the shame and become perfect and shameless (yet the self-doubt is still there; it's just suppressed). You don't need me to tell you which path you took.

Many people confuse guilt with shame and use the two words interchangeably. While at a quick glance they may look the same, they are very different (unlike shame, guilt *can* be measured; it is called a polygraph test). To put it simply, guilt is feeling bad about what you do, shame is feeling bad about who you are. In other words, guilt is about doing, shame is about being. When it comes to perfection we can dance between the two, but I find perfectionists tend to tango a lot more frequently with shame.

Fishkin explains that guilt is cerebral and cognitive and triggers an adrenal reaction when we realize we did something wrong. It stems from our intellect and is focused on our actions. Shame, however, is not an intellectual but rather a visceral reaction. It is internally focused and stems from who we think we are, versus the actions we take. As I glance back through my past, I can count on one hand the times I remember feeling guilty for my actions. The first one that always comes to mind is when I was I caught for stealing a bag of candy from my local candy store (ultimately an experience that served me well as I never stole anything again). However, I can easily recall hundreds of moments when a wave of shame came rushing over me due to feeling as though I was not measuring up somehow.

I can still remember vividly and viscerally the feeling I would experience when a panic attack would hit me out of nowhere. I would be sitting somewhere, talking to another person or a group, and out of nowhere my chest would tighten and my stomach would clench, signaling the coming attack. My first response was always to be angry and ashamed with myself for not being able to get a grip on the feelings as they gained momentum inside my body. Thinking that by shaming the rumblings I could make them go away, I tried everything I could to downgrade them. (You can imagine how well that went.) I would freeze in place and hold my breath while trying to search for an escape—the very thing I should not have done. In less than sixty seconds my entire body would be drenched in sweat, bringing on a visible display of embarrassment that I could no longer hide.

While I always felt a deep sense of anxiety around my panic attacks, the other, more painful piece of my perfection package was the shame it was wrapped in. The shame that I felt after yet another public reveal of my anxiety was quite possibly worse than the panic attack itself.

After each panic attack the internal verbal beating would begin. What was wrong with me? I'd ask myself. Why couldn't I get over this already? I couldn't see that the panic attacks were my body's desperate call for help and with each episode, the aftermath of the shame I felt would seep deeper into my psyche. It would take me years to arrive at a method for dealing with my emotions and the embarrassment that they caused.

It happened in a hotel lobby in Chicago, where I was enjoying a break between sessions at the fitness convention where I was presenting. Suddenly, I spotted my dermatologist, who happened to be attending a medical convention of her own. We had become friends after she saved my life by discovering a melanoma on my foot two years earlier. I don't know why seeing her brought on a panic attack—maybe because it brought back bad memories, maybe because seeing her out of the context made me feel displaced and therefore out of control. I couldn't figure it out but I forced myself to say hello to her. The anxiety continued to well up inside, until sud-denly, before I even had a chance to consciously consider what to do next, I blurted out: "It's so great to see you, but I think I may be having an anxiety attack. Do you mind if we just keep talking? It will eventually go away."

And boom, right there the battle was over. My chest relaxed, my stomach un-curled, my shoulders dropped, my perspiration ceased. It turned out that for me, all I had to do to reassert control of my body is to acknowledge that it was out of my control. Something about saying it out loud did the trick. Putting words to what I was experiencing removed the feeling of shame that was deeply interwoven into my anxiety and by doing so sucked the air out of my pending panic attack. The moment I faced and shared my fear, and acknowledged what I felt was my greatest physical flaw, the power of the overwhelming emotion driving it disappeared. My embarrass-ment had been acknowledged and my anxiety disappeared. With the snap of a finger, it was gone.

I am not suggesting that this is a one-size-fits-all solution to dealing with panic attacks, or the larger issue of shame. Panic attacks, especially if they are recurring, may require behavioral therapy and/or medication. I needed medication initially to help control them, and they wouldn't have gone away completely without behavioral therapy and adjustment. But I highlight this moment with my dermatologist because it was life-changing and proved to be pivotal in helping me detox from perfectionism. It also revealed to me that one of the paths to perfectionism recovery is found in the simple yet profound act of acknowledgment.

By seeing and speaking to our lack of control over everything, we place the parts of ourselves that we used to consider flawed into the light. In doing so, we rebuild our self-esteem and self-worth. Slowly, thought by positive thought, we strengthen our inner courage, enabling our lives to be lived with authenticity and bravery.

Not all feelings of shame are as easily identifiable or as situational. There are those, which I mentioned earlier, with much deeper roots and likely long-ago origins. These feelings typically originate in our childhood or teenage years, and their source must be sought or even coaxed out. Find the source and you will have identified your shame story. Confront the story, and you will be able to uproot the weeds of your past that caused much of your silent pain.

EVERY SHAME HAS A STORY

Our shame stories form early in our childhood, and no one gets through childhood unscathed or without being shamed. Does a story immediately come to mind for you? Or maybe this is something you have to sit with for a while before your story emerges. In either case, it's important to pause here and take a deep inhale as even thoughts of shame can create shallow breathing, a shutting off of sorts. Now, exhale from the knowingness that every healthy human feels or has felt shame at one time or another, it is just to what degree and what, if any, residue is left behind.

There is not a child I know who hasn't heard at some point, "I expected better of you!" or has witnessed a parent shake their head in disapproval. The natural and healthy reaction to these types of situations is to feel ashamed. If the parent or role model shares why they were disappointed and then follows up with a hug and piece of advice that is wrapped in love and a teachable moment, all is well and good. However, if the experience that caused the child to feel embarrassed or ashamed is not resolved in a healthy way, the shame will take root and work its way toward our self-esteem, where it can begin to do some damage. Shame, when not addressed in the present, will become a source of pain in the future.

Shame researcher Gershen Kaufman explains why shame is so hard to face: "Shame is the most disturbing experience individuals ever have about themselves: no other emotion feels more disturbing because in the moment of shame the self feels wounded from within."

While in therapy I could talk about my childhood and the pressures I felt in my career, I rarely if ever shared the moments in my life that caused me to feel ashamed. I would reveal all the other aspects in my life that I felt contributed to my perfectionism, but the stories that triggered my shame were so deeply uncomfortable to look at that I would just ignore them. As with any negative emotion that is silenced, the toxic residue began to seep into my life.

While I talked about my father I never really addressed the shame I felt in being the daughter of an alcoholic. As a child, I thought I was the only one in our town who had a father who would fall in the street, and I couldn't separate myself from his actions. It was as though I was the one drinking, and the embarrassment and shame

I felt was overwhelming at times. I experienced feelings of shame again when my teacher looked at my newly pierced ears and told me I looked like a slut. That moment caused me so much embarrassment that the negative feelings around my looks stayed with me for decades to come. And the shame I felt when a choreographer told me—in front of the entire dance company—that I could lose a few pounds would sit in my soul unaddressed for years to follow.

Shame is rarely a topic we bring up at dinner conversation or even with our closest friends, and so it sits festering in the dark recesses of our soul. We think we are the only ones who feel this way, and so we keep our doubts and demons to ourselves and let the layers of self-judgment pile on.

It was only last year that Lisa, my best friend of twenty-five years, and I talked about our own shame stories. We were at a Broadway play and during the intermission I was telling her about this chapter and the weight of shame residing in the perfectionist's soul. Organically we began to share our childhood stories that brought up memories of embarrassment. With tears in our eyes, we revealed the parts of our inner lives that had been left out of our conversations (and we have had thousands), as we felt too ashamed to reveal "that" part of ourselves, even with our best friend.

I never thought Lisa had dealt with any issues around shame. She always seemed so in control of her life and confident. I knew of her struggles as she knew of mine and while she openly admitted to being a perfectionist, many of her personality traits worked extremely well for her profession. She is in production and has an impeccable eye for detail. She will review programs and projects with a fine-toothed comb before signing off on them, and she mentors up-and-coming fitness professionals so masterfully that the young instructors she works with excel in their careers. In her personal life, she is a fantastic friend. She came to every one of my chemotherapy sessions and was so mad at herself the one time she showed up an imperfect ten minutes late, due to an unforeseeable train delay. Lisa is a loving and caring wife and is deeply respected by all who know her. She has worked hard to let go of the parts of perfectionism that no longer serve her and has kept the traits that do.

Lisa's struggle with perfectionism has been a journey and in her past it had a very dark side. Bulimia, anorexia, and at times, deep self-doubt that plagued her on the inside. Lisa and I had talked frequently about my work and her own struggles with perfection, but it wasn't until we were talking in the lobby of the Broadway show that I understood both the root of her perfectionism and the shame that drove it into full-throttle mode.

One day when Lisa was in college, her father, whom she adored and to this day has a beautiful relationship with, discovered she was having sex with her boyfriend.

In his discomfort and probably embarrassment he uttered one sentence, "You are no longer special." It took less than two seconds to say, but that sentence lingered in the air for the next decade. The shame that washed over Lisa because of her father's stinging disapproval was never addressed. Lisa began to try to reclaim being the perfect daughter by doing what else—being perfect. Lisa was a phenomenal dancer and, like me, her perfectionism and false sense of control took root through her body, what she ate, how much she exercised, and how she looked.

Many years later, Lisa choreographed a dance piece that was based in the pain that this moment with her father had caused. As Lisa danced, moved, and flowed through the air, her body released the hurt that her heart could not hold onto any longer. The silence of shame that she had held for so many years was broken at the end of her piece. Lisa stopped, paused, looked up and out into the audience, and repeated that one sentence "You are no longer special."

In the audience that day was Lisa's father. After her performance they went for a walk. With tears in his eyes, he suddenly stopped and turned to his beautiful daughter, "I had no idea that I caused you so much pain; I was just trying to protect my baby girl. I am so deeply sorry." In that moment, Lisa's shame was seen and spoken to, and it was only then that it could be released.

A TALE OF TOO MUCH LIP SERVICE

Peter was his name. He was a tall skinny kid who had little in the way of social skills and who had decided that I was going to be his target. "Luscious lips" he would call me. "Look at her and her luscious lips!" he would taunt. OK, to be honest, if someone said that to me now I would be thrilled, but as an eight-year-old it made me feel different, and at that age all we want to do is blend in.

My mouth was one that most plastic surgeons these days would charge thousands of dollars to create, but as a child I hated standing out. If I knew then what I know now, I would have told my mum that Peter had made me feel bad and hurt my feelings. That would have released my pain and by doing so that moment, while uncomfortable, would have been done and dusted. As lead shame researcher Brené Brown reminds us, "When we can share our story with someone who responds with empathy and understanding, shame can't survive." Shame thrives in isolation and dies in connection.

But at eight years old, I didn't know any better, and, instead of embracing my full mouth and telling Peter off, I felt as though I must be doing something wrong to be noticed. I would cover my face with my hand as I spoke, purse my lips to try and make them smaller, and go out of my way to downplay how I looked. I felt such deep shame around looking different that I missed out on the natural part of being a teenager. Instead of blooming, I would cut myself down as much as I could.

(As a side note: In my early twenties I was hired as a lip model for a national drink commercial, and for one ten-second spot, those luscious lips made over $30,000. Boom. Take that, Peter.)

WHEN SHAME MADE THE FRONT PAGE NEWS

Shame runs deep and can wash over us at any moment. When a secret becomes public or an old wound is brought to the surface, shame will be waiting for us. We often segment our lives into small pieces and compartmentalize the parts that seem unlovable or different. I met Rocky when I was still presenting at fitness conventions. She was a fantastic instructor but an even better compartmentalization expert. In compartment one was the outgoing and fun-loving fitness instructor. In compartment two was the mother of two teenage boys and wife to a loving husband. In compartment three was the secret that both her sons struggled with mental health issues and in compartment four was the stress of over $300,000 in medical bills that were not covered by insurance. Over the years Rocky had learned how to navigate the healthcare system and help her boys rise from the ashes more than once, but no one had taught Rocky how to exist when all her compartments came crashing down.

Rocky began raising funds for causes around mental health issues by starting a fitness fundraiser called Stomp Out The Stigma. For the first few years she kept a distance between her life story and the fundraisers. No one knew that Rocky's family was in the midst of their own crisis around the stigma of mental health challenges, after all how would that reflect on her image as the perfect fitness instructor?

Slowly the distance between the perfect life that she was presenting on the outside and the daily struggles tugging at her insides became too big to compartmentalize. She began having frequent panic attacks and on occasion the stress became so overwhelming that her body would go into anaphylactic shock.

Rocky knew something had to change and so along with beginning to share her backstory with those closest to her, she also became a behavioral health advocate, raising her voice for those who couldn't. As her role expanded she was invited to speak at some high-profile meetings and organizations. However one day and without realizing it, a meeting was being recorded and soon her compartments were going to be blown wide open.

December 21, 2015, was just another normal winter day until Rocky picked up the local paper and without any warning or approval on the front page were all the details about Rocky's family. The private information that Rocky had shared at a recent government meeting was now in public for everyone to see.

Her stomach tightened and a wave of hot red shame washed over her as she saw her name, where she lived, her struggles, and her story spread across the local newspaper. Now everyone knew, everyone including the next-door neighbor, the teachers, the grocery store owners—everyone.

After a few days of trying to stay low and out of sight, Rocky decided she would have to finally step out to get some much-needed groceries. Still covered in a blanket of shame she was holding her breath just waiting for the looks, the whispers, and the knowing glances to begin. But that never happened. Instead people from all walks of life, some she knew and many she didn't, came up to her and thanked her for being so brave. Some would share their own struggles along with words of appreciation for the information that was shared in the article on where to get help.

Shame has no filter, it is a fast-flowing reaction to everything we feel is not perfect in our lives. Yet when we can peek under the hood of shame we will find worn-out stories that no longer serve us or our mission to leave the world a better place.

Rocky's shame was washed away by the love and gratitude of all the people she was helping. If she had kept her struggles a secret, she would still be living in the darkness of shame and solitude. Rocky decided to turn pain into her calling. She is now a leading behavioral health advocate who is on a mission to create more health resources to address mental illness. Rocky is now frequently invited to speak on the subject and just recently was invited to the White House to share her story.

Your detox for today is to recognize that we all feel moments of shame and that this is OK. What's not OK is continuing to push them away. It's time to look your shame in the eye and tolerate the icky feelings that arise; only this act will weaken this powerful emotion. Sitting with and settling with your shame will allow you to get to the other side, and open the doorway for your best self to make an entrance. It will be a radical and possibly challenging step, but one of the most rewarding shifts you can make.

Daily Detox

1. Spend some time noticing which part of your perfectionism triggers a feeling of embarrassment or shame most often. Choose only one trigger and write it down. For Rocky, it was the shame of pretending her life was perfect each time she taught a fitness class. For me, it was the shame that came up right after a panic attack.

2. Find an artistic outlet to release your shame story around this trigger. For Lisa, it was dancing, for Rocky it was Zumba, for me it was writing. For you, it could be dance as well, or maybe painting, drawing, or journaling about how you feel will create the best release for you. You can also create a collage of pictures and words—when was the last time you sat down with a bunch of magazines and ripped out things that spoke to you? This tactile experience, i.e., one that does not involve electronics, will be grounding, even if you focus it on the topic of shame. Whatever medium you choose, remember that the intention of this exercise is not to create something beautiful or share-worthy, it's simply an outlet for your story. This may take a while and I encourage you to take your time with it; it doesn't have to be done in one session.

3. Fess up about your struggles with the shame that is wrapped around your perfectionism with someone you trust not to judge you. Remember trust needs to be earned, and sharing your shame story with an empathetic friend, sibling, or even parent is a powerful step to stopping the shame game. More than likely the person you choose to trust with your story will have a story of their own to share in return.

4. Every time you feel that wave of shame wash over you when you *think* you've failed to do something or show up "perfectly," stop and give yourself a hug. I mean a literal hug. It will bring attention to how quickly we judge ourselves, and a hug is an act of radical self-love and self-acceptance. Besides, hugs release oxytocin, which is the love drug, so not only will you decrease the impact of the shame wave, you will also increase the stimulation of your "feel good" nervous center.

PART TWO

SHIFT YOUR FOCUS
AND LIVE BRAVELY

STEP 8

Welcome a Misstep as an Opportunity to Explore, Learn, and Engage

B Y NOW YOU HAVE GONE THROUGH A NUMBER OF DETOX STEPS AND HOPEFULLY YOU'RE feeling some relief from the burden of perfectionism. If at this point you are still feeling the weight on your shoulders, trust the process and your inner wisdom, and know that this next phase of the program will continue to work toward relieving some of that pressure. Be sure to keep in mind that there is no way to do this detox perfectly and the process will be different for everyone. Just as there is not a one-size-fits-all diet or workout program, this detox will unfold in a way that is best for you and your life.

Regardless of what steps you've completed up until now, I want to remind you of an essential point, something that I hope you will always keep at the forefront of your mind and present in your heart. And that point is this: perfectionism does not have to be a curse and you are already, just as you are, an incredible human being (we'd be BFFs for sure). There is a lot to admire about you, and I have no doubt that you were a rock star the day you picked up this book. Perhaps you may have lost sight of your inner awesomeness, but you are a rock star nonetheless, and I want to work with you to bring some of your greatness back into focus.

Remember that as a perfectionist, you do have some advantages. For example, you probably excel (even though you might not think so) at what you do professionally, or as a hobby, and there's a good chance you leave a mark of excellence on even one-time endeavors. In fact, you are likely much better and more successful at anything you try than you think you are and you have many wonderful characteristics.

Yet, you may be one of the most unfulfilled people you know. Don't despair; it isn't because you are not worthy of feeling at ease and content, although my guess is that this is a recurrent thought for you. Rather it is because you are trapped in a cycle that includes focusing on the parts of your life that do not move you into a joyful state, working to meet unrealistic expectations around success, and seeing failure where there is none. This cycle has likely paralyzed you into what is essentially a state of perpetual discomfort, a state dominated by the sense of dread that you are failing and letting everyone, including yourself, down. The culprit behind this humming sense of dread is the undercurrent of low-grade fear that has been your constant, if quiet companion. For a perfectionist, the fear of failure, or even the possibility of failing to reach your goal on perfect terms, scares you profoundly. So intense is this fear that it will ultimately derail you from the path of living up to your potential—and enjoying the rewards.

In this step, we will talk about missteps and mistakes, these unavoidable facets of existence that we perfectionists believe we can, through use of our unique powers, evade. But we can't. And if we do somehow manage to accomplish this evasion, we will do so at a substantial personal cost. As author J. K. Rowling (who by the way had her Harry Potter manuscript rejected by *twelve* publishers before one saw its potential) reminds us: "It is impossible to live without failing at something, unless you live so cautiously that you might as well not have lived at all, in which case you have failed by default."

LEARNING TO LIVE WITH FAILURE

Tal Ben-Shahar, one of my teachers and the author of a best-selling book on perfectionism, says that to avoid the predicament of the permanent pause—that is, the state in which we can be frozen if we let our fears of not achieving the ideal outcome stay in the driver's seat—perfectionists must either "learn to fail" or "fail to learn."

By failing to learn, Ben-Shahar means that your inability to accept failure as a possibility will in the long run prevent you from taking the necessary risks to achieve your goals, to move ahead, and to get better. This is the reason that for most perfectionists, stagnation is inevitable, and with long-term stagnation they run the risk of keeping their ideas, dreams, and authentic voice hidden from the world.

The trouble is that we often think by playing it safe that we will indeed reach great heights, but that is just another lie that our inner critic tells us daily. Trying to protect us, she keeps us doubting our worth and prevents us from sharing our unique points of view and the best parts of ourselves because we may be judged or criticized. Think about someone in your life who once showed so much potential, but to your surprise—and to surprise of many—became burned out and/or never reached their goals. No doubt, that person personified many features of the perfectionist model. The all-or-nothing mindset can lead to nothing.

It is hard to remember—especially when you are in the throes of perfectionism—that mistakes or missteps are only proof that you've pushed limits, tried harder, and thought bigger. Failure is inevitable during such attempts, but because perfectionists see any failure, real or perceived, as an all-encompassing action as opposed to a single event, they avoid it at all costs. We see failure, when it happens, as part of our identity, a reflection of who we are versus an action we took. But if you consider failure not as an outcome to be avoided but as First Attempts In Learning, your perception of the event will undergo a radical transformation. While I don't believe in failing my way to the top, I do believe failure is an unavoidable part of the road to success.

FREEING YOURSELF FROM A FIXED MINDSET

As a public speaker, my biggest fear was being asked a question while I was on stage and not knowing the answer. Despite all the energy and anxiety, the sweat and tears invested in this fear over the years, this scenario has actually only happened to me once. Still: that *one time* has haunted me for twenty years. To this day, I recall with remarkable though unnecessary detail the event, where it took place (New York City), what the question was, and who (it was my friend Annie) asked it. That's how deeply etched a misstep, or a failure to immediately provide an accurate answer, became in my perfectionistic mind.

The fact that in preparing for the presentation I didn't anticipate *all* possible outcomes and questions that could arise gnawed on me for months. Until a simple awareness dawned on me—it is not humanly possible to (1) Anticipate all possible questions, and (2) Know the answers to them. A recent lunch with Annie revealed to me how unnecessary my self-castigation had been. It turns out that my failure to provide an answer to Annie's question that has so gnawed on me didn't even register in her memory. When I brought up the moment that occurred in the late nineties (don't judge), which had haunted me for so many years, she had no idea what I was talking about; she didn't even remember being at that specific event.

These days I welcome all questions at my seminars. Most of the time I have an answer that feels on point, but occasionally I get stumped. However, I now view such moments as opportunities to learn something new, to explore different angles on a topic that I may not have considered before, and to expand my knowledge. If I don't know the answer, I am comfortable saying so, or I use my virtual assistant Google to provide me with a little background on a topic so I can engage in the discussion. I always promise to do some research into the subject and follow up if possible.

Are there still instances when I don't know the answer? You bet. But usually someone in the audience knows, and I welcome their input without seeing it as a personal assault on my authority as a speaker. I thank them sincerely. Often, such turns help me to form a tighter bond with my audience, and the audience appreciates the event more because they feel like they have contributed some value to the process. It makes them see the experience as a conversation rather than an impersonal lecture and Q&A.

This change of mindset—from fearing to embracing the possibility of failure—is something that psychologist and author Carol Dweck, Ph.D., refers to as going from a "fixed" to a "growth" mindset. If your mindset is "fixed" you may attain your goal of living a mistake-, misstep-, and failure-free life, but at a staggering cost to your potential and your purpose. As you dodge the risk of failure by limiting your choices, you also miss the opportunities to expand your knowledge, options, networks, and fulfillment.

Eventually, your tolerance for risk lowers to such an extent that any possibility for growth is all but whittled away. Your sphere will gradually shrink, while your attitude will grow more judgmental of others, especially of those who, by taking risks, will eventually surpass you. Rest assured they will have made many mistakes, while you didn't, but as a reward they will soar to greater heights while you will, at best, continue to cruise at steady altitude.

HOW PROGRESS HAPPENS IN THE GREAT LAB OF LIFE

There is a great freedom that comes with learning to shift our thought process around making mistakes and adjusting our definition of failure. When we learn to view mishaps not as failures but as stepping-stones to something bigger and better we begin to access our inner courage versus our inner critic. Just remind yourself that many of the world's greatest inventions were mistakes that happened in the lab. The Slinky. Post-it Notes. Penicillin! These are just some of the wonderful things that came from mistakes.

Most if not all top leaders have learned the art of maneuvering through their mistakes and surviving (perceived) failure. In a recent interview on the *CBS This Morning* news show, Sarah Robb O'Hagan, CEO of Flywheel Sports and a friend of mine, was asked whether she thought people learned more from success or failure. Sarah openly discussed her failures, even epic ones, in her book *Extreme You*, so you can probably guess her answer . . . in response, she said that it was in her failures that her greatest lessons originated. It was also in these moments that she learned the depth of her grit, resilience, and tenacity, all necessary assets to living bravely and boldly.

In an article in *Fast Company*, Amazon founder Jeff Bezos shared that one of the reasons his company is excelling is because they are willing to embrace uncertainty, experimentation, and messy inconsistencies. He said that not everything at Amazon is orchestrated for perfection. Bezos doesn't only tolerate mistakes, he enjoys them and sees them as another source from which a brand new idea may arise.

At this moment, you may be rolling your eyes and saying to yourself, "Well, that is all very well and good, but Amazon is a huge company and Sarah is chatting it up on CBS. They've already made it and so can afford to make mistakes" . . . but you are looking at their "overnight" success instead of their ten-thousand-hour-long journey. You don't learn to operate with their degree of internal strength in a short period of time; it's a process of growth that requires developing not just a solid through-line of trust in yourself, but also a trust in the evolutionary process that must occur for progress to happen.

To look at it another way, they've learned to accept the fact that long-lasting success is never linear. It consists of many mini wins and then an epic fail, of having to hear "no" ten times before you hear one "yes." For perfectionists, this is an extremely uncomfortable reality to accept. What I've learned, however, is that we can train our brains to sit in the discomfort, and this will allow for the lessons we need to learn to reveal themselves. In these lessons, you will find the catalysts to success.

TAKING STEPS TOWARD LIVING BRAVELY

If you want to live more joyfully, you must begin living bravely. To live bravely means being willing to try and fail and try again.

These days, failure means one thing to me: not trying. If I were to not go for an interview or take on a speaking gig because I was afraid of making a mistake, or if I opted out of trying a new keynote because I was afraid it wouldn't go flawlessly, that would be failure in my book. Making a mistake used to terrify me; now it's the idea of going to my grave saying "what if" that scares me more than anything. What I want more now than ever is to be a student of life, to keep learning and searching new and different ways to motivate and inspire my audiences. And each time I learn something new, I can guarantee that my future is going to be riddled with mistakes and flops and also with renewed excitement, curiosity, and enthusiasm for my life. I will take that trade-off anytime.

Sometimes what's more challenging than learning something new is testing out your new skills, as was the case for Laurie. I met Laurie at my first-ever Perfection Detox workshop. She was a highly respected and seasoned trainer who had been teaching spin classes for over twenty years. Laurie loved her job but had recently begun to feel a little burned out due to instructing the same type of class for over two decades.

Over the past five years Laurie had taken and passed (with flying colors) almost every single fitness certification there was to take. While she had the proof that she was prepared and ready, Laurie had never gotten over her fear that her first "new" class may not be the "perfect" new class. She had the skills, she had the certifications, but she was being suffocated by the false fears that come with perfection. The fear that if something is not perfect, then it was a failure, and so while Laurie kept on achieving certification after certification, she only recently decided to put her new skill set into action.

During the workshop while discussing fear, and that the brain cannot tell the difference between fact and fiction, Laurie brought up the overwhelming anxiety that would wash over her anytime she placed her skills and reputation on the line by trying something new. Fact one was that even though Laurie had been teaching only indoor cycling for twenty years, her teaching skills would cross over into all types of fitness classes. The second fact was that Laurie was an excellent student and had already mastered the key elements she would need to teach a different style of class. Fact three was that Laurie was always prepared, and we knew that she would practice, practice, practice to make sure she was ready for any type of class that she would be instructing. The last fact was that Laurie's students and clients loved her and many had followed her from gym to gym over the years. Laurie could have taught a class on basket weaving and they would have all showed up.

The reality was that while teaching a new format would of course be a little anxiety provoking, Laurie had all the skills necessary to make any "new" class a fantastic experience for her students. On looking back she could see that her anxiety was a sign of how much she cared about her members and that fear was a signal that she was stretching both herself and her comfort zone.

We talked through the emotions that would come up anytime she was going to teach a new fitness format. The night before, her false fears would creep in and she would always have doubts about her skill set and second thoughts about her decision. But the moment the music started, Laurie would drop into her comfort zone of being a seasoned instructor and love every moment of teaching the new class.

Were there a few mishaps? Possibly, but none that her students noticed and nothing came up that she couldn't work around using her twenty-plus years of teaching experience. Laurie shared with me that while she had decided to keep her indoor cycling classes as her main format, she now felt confident that she could successfully, and even joyfully, teach other types of fitness classes should she decide to.

You, too, can implement steps that will help introduce a similar change in mindset or embolden you to take a leap, no matter what the consequences. You can work on dissecting fact from fiction, as I had Laurie do. Or you can also take another series of steps that can recalibrate your risk tolerance.

The first step is to shift your beliefs around mistakes and perceived failures by changing your definition of what these two words mean to you. What would happen if you saw mistakes as information and data? How would your world open up if you viewed your failures as success catalysts? I've learned that I garner a great deal more usable information from my mistakes than from my successes, and that this information often allows me to grow or branch out in ways I would have never anticipated.

The next step is to downgrade the power of praise. This means allowing yourself a small celebration when you feel you've mastered the moment, but then separating the praise from your ego. Establishing a separation between what we do and who we are is important for perfectionists during good times, and the not-so-good times when we might endure punishment instead of praise from our ego. It's a separation that allows us to acknowledge that while we will make mistakes, we are not the mistake. It also allows us to shake off the emotions of shame and guilt that inevitably come knocking when mistakes are made or mishaps occur.

For most perfectionists, when we give it our all and show up fully, and a mistake happens, we have a difficult time seeing it as just that: a mistake. We've been programmed to overlook or reject situational explanations that might make other people feel better about a slipup. But in our day-to-day misses, it is important to remember that when the intention is good and we have given it our all, guilt and shame are inappropriate responses. They will never help us improve, in fact they will more than likely stop us from trying again in the future, as the toxic feelings that come with those emotions are too uncomfortable to bear.

Adopting a more rational view of the consequences of failure can also help move us into the land of living bravely. You can invite this shift in simply by paying attention to your own learned response to making mistakes and pausing to consider whether the reaction is appropriate to the size of error made.

For example, think about the last time you made a typo and hit send, or the last time you forgot a work colleague's birthday. Or any other "mistake" that every single one of us has made at some point and will probably make again in the future. How loud is the voice of your inner critic when those types of errors happen? Being slightly annoyed with yourself for a second or two is fine, even reasonable, shaming yourself for the next twenty-four hours and beyond is not.

Fear also plays a big part in reframing the failure mindset. Particularly with perfectionists the fear of not living up to other people's expectations can be debilitating. Seth Godin, the author of eighteen international bestsellers, including *Tribes*, said that to be remarkable you need to be remarked upon. This means that people will remark on what they like about you *and* what they don't. It's certainly easier to hear the former rather than the latter, but even that means you are being noticed. When you are living bravely, you can take this as an acknowledgment that you are being heard without feeling the need to modify your message to gain other people's approval. My friend Jenny Blake, author and fellow recovering perfectionist, told me that when she feels the need for other people's approval beginning to take center stage, she quietly says to herself, "I am not here to audition for other people's lives."

If our idea of success is always about proving our worth and always being right, then we are in for a lot of headaches and heartbreak. When success is tied to the outcome it is a thin tightrope we walk filled with tension and stress. Instead, we should aim to stay buoyant during the times of struggle, see the ebbs and flows as a part of the process of growth, proof that we are living, loving, and most importantly, trying.

We can still identify the parts of ourselves or skills that need to be strengthened, but we can view them instead as opportunities to learn and grow, and we can use the success of those around us as motivation to fill our own inspiration tank instead of feeling threatened by their wins.

Daily Detox

Today, and in the days to come, try doing the following to adjust your failure perception:

1. If someone makes a reference to a name, occurrence, or place you don't know, just say honestly that you don't get the reference and ask her to explain it to you. If it makes you feel better, say you wish

you knew the reference, but you don't. Ask to be enlightened. This small step will improve communication while also building a renewed sense of collaboration.

2. If you prepare for a presentation or a public event, set a reasonable time limit for this effort. Don't try to explore *all* possible angles and questions prior to the event. I promise that whatever you lose in what you perceive as the optimal "quality" of the presentation you'll make up in the good spirit with which you approach the task. And people will relate to you better. (Remember that people don't relate to "flawless" as intimately as they do to the "authentic.")

3. One day this week, stretch yourself outside of your comfort zone. Is there something at work you would like to learn how to do? Is there a project you have not started because you needed to ask for help but were afraid to do so? Or maybe you have wanted to begin drawing, take a pottery class, or start dancing but held back because you didn't want to play the part of the beginner. No more waiting—this week is the week to find your inner Picasso or Ginger Rogers. After you have picked out the activity, and taken the first step to fulfilling it, write it down in your journal, and record your impressions as you delve in more deeply. If you decide not to pursue, figure out why, and try something else. Keep going until you find something you can stick with.

Clean Up Your Vocabulary: Replace "No, but . . . " with "Yes, and . . . "

PERFECTIONISTS LIVE IN THE WORLD WHERE EVERYTHING IS EITHER BLACK OR WHITE, PERFECT or imperfect, good or bad, right or wrong. We see our relationships and outcomes as either successes or failures, and our destination as either inevitable or impossible. Perfectionists are also prone to dwelling in the land of preemptive disillusionment, where expectations of the worst reign supreme. Even once an event or experience has passed, we are more likely to reflect with a "What if?" rather than to exclaim "How good was that!"

The problem with living on this planet of absolutes, where black and white thinking rules over all, is that it's lonely, and out of touch with the complexities—and the color—of real life. In this step, I want to help you move from this lonely planet to a place where white bleeds into black, and where we might even see red and blue and pink all over. Getting there requires shifting your focus from life's narrow flaws to its abundant possibilities, an adjustment that can be made in part by utilizing the power of language, specifically by rethinking the words "no," "but," "yes," and "and." These may be small words, but they are mighty and have a surprising degree of influence on whether you take advantage of, or surrender, the power of choice.

DISPATCHES FROM THE LONELY PLANET OF NO

The first phrase I want to invite you to drop from your vocabulary is, "No, but . . . " I'm referring to these words as you might use them when a friend asks you to a dinner party (and you are having a fat day or a bad hair day): "No, but I would have loved to if I were available." Or when you've been asked to try out an activity you've never done before (and you are not sure if you will enjoy or be successful at it): "No, but next time for certain." Or when you're thinking of sharing the project you've been working on: "No, but when it is ready (meaning perfect) I will show you."

If your first impulse is to always say "no" to an opportunity and think about it later, consider saying "yes" instead. I am not suggesting that you mindlessly accept something you shouldn't; in fact, knowing how to say "no" to joy-sucking propositions is a positive ability, especially if you are prone to people-pleasing behaviors. What I am suggesting is that you work on not saying no simply because you can't count on a specific outcome. You can accomplish this by (1) not reflexively slamming every unexpected door that's opened to you, and (2) shifting your focus to the opportunity that's presenting itself. Consider this an invitation to say "yes" before you think you are ready, *and* to embrace the potential upside before there is any guarantee there will be one.

At first this will seem scary and unnatural because you've been using "no" and "but" as opt-outs, and as a means of protection. In fact, these words are a perfectionist's—and a procrastinator's—escape route of choice. We convince ourselves that the "no" + "but" combo softens the blow of rejection or allows us to avert the possibility of failure, but this exit strategy locks us out of life, eliminating unique experiences and opportunities for growth. The real issue arises when "no" becomes our default to the point that is a bona fide behavioral habit.

My big "no, but" moment happened many years ago when CBS invited me to be the fitness expert on their New Year's Resolution show. My initial reply was, "I'd love to be on your show, *but* I'm already booked that day." That "but" was my way to soften the refusal and was also a lie. My schedule was wide open, but the thought of not looking perfect and making a flawless appearance on a live television show seemed too overwhelming. With my habitual response, I once again boxed myself into the small world of "no, but."

I had been saying "no" so frequently over the prior two years that every time I turned down another opportunity I pushed it aside, never discussed it, and with each "no" another piece of my self-esteem was being chipped away. However, on this particular morning in December something amazing happened. My inner wisdom, the part of me that knew that this was an opportunity I needed to grab, stood up and spoke up. Hope beat fear, and in that moment, the rumblings of my inner critic were silenced and my life began to open up to possibility.

Between the time I said "No, I am booked already (lie), but I'd love to be your guest next time," to the time I called them back to say, "I changed my schedule (lie) and yes, I would love to do the show," the spot was still vacant. I was extremely lucky as the list of people for that type of national appearance was long, and filled with very talented individuals. This was a transformational moment; when I said "yes" to the show, I was also saying "yes" to my life. I said yes before I was ready *and* I knew that I would figure out the details as to not let CBS or myself down.

After wrapping up my "yes" call with CBS, I had two weeks in which to get ready for this new opportunity, which was both exhilarating and terrifying. I knew I couldn't prepare for this alone and so I called my old therapist. With her help, along with some mindfulness techniques, I felt secure in the fact that I could manage my anxiety. I kept reminding myself that anxiety was just excitement without the breath. This helped as it enabled me to reframe what I was feeling (crazy butterflies in my stomach) from a negative to a positive. In addition, I prepared, prepared, and then prepared some more. I knew that live TV was anything but predictable, and this meant that the more I rehearsed, the more I could be in the moment, spontaneous, and ready to go with the flow. And there was a chance that I would even have fun, too! Was the show perfect? I didn't think so but I had a terrific time, and I did a good enough job that over the next two years I become a regular fitness expert on the show.

A young poet named Erin Hanson once wrote, "There is a freedom waiting for you, on the breezes of the sky, and you ask, 'What if I fall?' Oh, but my darling, 'What if you fly?'" Of course, if you want to fly, you have to first give yourself the chance to do so by taking to the sky.

To get there, you must surrender "no, but" to the leap-inspiring word of "yes." "Yes" gives you that chance to fly, before you are ready. It is about saying "yes" to an interview, even if you are not sure that you are the best candidate for the job, or that the job is a perfect one for you. It is about saying "yes" to the blind date, even when you feel a little overweight. It is putting the camera down and saying "yes" to being in the photo, even when you are not feeling your perfect self. No longer will you need to wait for the perfect moment, the perfect weight, the perfect situation, or for everything to be just right for you to begin. Because you know what? Those moments never arrive.

CREATING A "YES" HABIT
(AND ENTERING THE LAND OF "AND")

When we can say "yes" every day and not just on the days where we feel perfect, our life begins to find color. We get to paint outside the lines and show a willingness to participate in our lives. ("Willingness" is a word that perfectionists rarely use as it opens us up to all of life and not only to the circumstances that we think we can control.) Through this act of participation we acknowledge that desire for perfection and acceptance of imperfection can coexist in a happy union, and this lays the groundwork for freedom and for brighter, fuller lives to flourish.

What "yes" does best is allow you to open up to curiosity and awe and begin to trigger more feel-good emotions; it gives you the chance to explore life instead of trying to control it. By saying yes, you put action to your intentions of detoxing from perfection; you give your thoughts legs, so to speak, and let them get to running.

When we marry the word "yes" with "and," we expand our opportunities even more and give ourselves breathing room to figure things out, ask for help, or do the research necessary to move our "yes" over the finish line. While "no, but" are woven together to offer a reason for declining the opportunity in front of us, while also trying to maintain the illusion of perfection, "and" is the silent promise we make to ourselves to show up for our "yes." This quiet, yet strong "and" is the loving commitment we make to ourselves to do the necessary work and put action behind our dreams. Saying "yes" is one thing; committing to our yes is another.

When we allow ourselves to be comfortable in the discomfort of realizing that we may not actually be ready for our yes just yet, we are able to work with grit and resilience and stay buoyant until we figure it out. Perfection cannot coexist with yes alone, as we will need to ask for help, research the details, and fill in our gaps to rise out of stagnation—and this is where the "and" comes in.

"And" is the inner work that we are prepared to do to meet our external "yes" with enthusiasm and determination. "And" shows a willingness to put some skin in the game and helps us to stop overthinking and start living. "And" allows you to say yes to life, and then figure out the details. If we wait until we think we are (perfectly) ready to begin something we will be missing countless opportunities.

The Roman philosopher Seneca said that luck is what happens when preparation meets opportunity. When we take advantage of "and" in our lives, we begin to create more of our own luck. Even though you don't have time, say yes to the blind date *and* while you may not find the love of your life, you may make a new friend who enjoys doing the same things as you do. Say yes to whatever it is that you have been putting off for the past year, *and* as you push yourself further than you thought you could your courage will get a positivity boost.

Even though you are exhausted, say yes to date night *and* you will remember why you fell in love with this person sitting across the restaurant table. Even though you don't think you will get it, say yes to the job interview *and* then ask for help to ensure you are prepared as possible. When you are feeling a little blue and think you should go to work, say yes to taking a mental health day, *and* know you are setting the new standards for what radical self-care means.

Say yes to you, to your life, to your dreams and while not everything may work out perfectly, the person you become along the way is worth every heartbreak, failure, disappointment, and imperfect moment.

Laurie, whom you met in the previous chapter, had been thinking about becoming a certified integrative nutrition coach so that she could broaden her skill set to include lifestyle and behavioral techniques. She knew that after twenty-plus years of teaching she needed to find a way to create income that was not always transactional based and that needed her to show up physically. Like most of us, Laurie was very comfortable staying in her lane but her children were now teenagers and she wanted to pursue new and meaningful goals to help prepare her transition to becoming an empty nester. In the last Perfection Detox workshop Laurie attended, we were exploring the ways we put our dreams on delay and she realized that her knee-jerk response to her big dreams was "no, but." That following week, after thinking things through and speaking with her husband, Laurie decided to say "yes, and" to her future.

Before she had figured out how she was going to make everything work, including navigating her family's busy schedules, organizing her current commitments, and making the time for an additional eight hours of studying per week, she said "yes" and signed up for a yearlong nutrition program, and then she began to plan out the details.

Had Laurie waited for the perfect time and the perfect situation to unfold before signing onto a yearlong program, well it would never have happened. Laurie shared that by taking care of her needs and pursuing her passion, she felt as though she was also able to be a more loving mother and wife for her family.

The word "and" allows us to move out of our black or white, all-or-nothing fixed mindset. We are able to adjust our language from absolutes such as success "or" failure or I am fit "or" fat, to a more tolerant and loving dialogue with ourselves. We discover that we can fail *and* learn valuable information through our mistakes that guarantees our success the next time around. And while we may not always be at our most fit when dating- or work-related opportunities appear, we can still go forward with energy *and* dress for success *and* bring our A game to the event.

We all know there is never a perfect time to start something; "Yes and" allows you to start before you are ready and in doing so your life will rise up to meet you in action.

One of the side-effects of perfectionism is procrastination. Procrastination protects us from being judged. We never get going, so we never complete the task and so we never have to show our work or our ideas. Procrastination happens when we spend too much time in our heads, mulling over the pros and cons, the risk versus the reward and we lose hours of our precious life trying to dodge the bullet of possible failure.

Most people think that motivation is what they need to stop procrastination in its tracks. However, if we wait for the motivation to arrive, we will never begin. Yes is the true way to tap into your intrinsic motivation to create a new way, a new routine, a new habit. Say "yes " and you will be amazed as to how much your motivation and zest for life will increase. Your readiness and enthusiasm to try new things will become stronger as you slowly build your new habit of "Yes."

LEARNING TO TAKE A CHANCE ON LOVE
(EVEN ON BAD HAIR DAYS)

"Yes" is a particularly difficult word for perfectionists when it comes to romantic relationships. Commitment aversion—overt or subconscious—to engagements, serious or casual, is another perfectionistic personality signature trait. (If you are wondering why, it is because no area of life is so fraught with landmines of unpredictability and uncontrollability than our love lives. And to perfectionists, surrendering control is tantamount to accepting unconditionally a less-than-perfect outcome.)

For example, prior to my perfection detox, I was reluctant to accept a date unless I knew that I would feel and look impeccable; that my clothes, makeup, and body mass index couldn't be better; that the chemistry between me and the potential date was palpable, our conversation sizzling, the setting romantic, and so forth. If any one of these seemed even slightly off kilter, my posture would droop with disappointment, I would take it on as my fault, and take myself out of the moment by starting to daydream about slipping into my PJs alone, at home with my bag of potato chips, endless sitcom reruns, and maybe that Chardonnay. To use a cooking metaphor, if one ingredient was missing, I was ready to discard the entire pot.

The perfectionist's discomfort with taking the plunge is a substantial disruptor to personal fulfillment. It is especially true when it comes to romantic relationships because this discomfort negates, preemptively, the possibility of the gratifying and joyful outcomes that love and companionship bring. Rather than accepting the possibility of a less-than-perfect setting or a perfect date with a simple "yes," the perfectionist opts for a more secure "no" and settles for the secure solitude. By rejecting the possibility of an exuberant "yes," she is cutting off, one day at a time, the path to satisfaction.

I remember one woman in the Perfection Detox workshop by the name of Lucy who reflected on how finite her perfectionist dating standard had become. She recalled how she once rejected an invitation to dinner with a man she was attracted to because it was a hot and humid day. I knew right away what Lucy meant: on a hot and humid day, she wouldn't look or feel her best. Her hair would frizz; the idea of perspiration would distract her from conversation. She would rather forgo the opportunity to get to know a man she likes than to allow him a glance at her bad hair day. Crazy, no?

Later, Lucy knew she had a breakthrough when she accepted a blind date on a day she knew would be hot and humid. She said yes, and had a great time. Not because she ended up marrying the man, but because saying "yes" and embracing an imperfect set of circumstances liberated her and strengthened her courage muscle.

STEPPING OFF THE SIDELINES, AND INTO THE GAME

In her book *Emotional Agility*, Susan David wrote about choosing courage over comfort. I used to use "no" as a protective shield and especially on the days I felt less than perfect, no was my first line of defense. No would keep me in the shadow of what I knew and would protect me from the risk of failure. No kept me safe and no kept me small. No kept me in my routine and also kept me from trying new things, meeting new people, and broadening my experiences while also building my courage.

There is also a healthy no that will rise up as you begin to reclaim your spontaneity and learn to live bravely. You will begin saying no to the people and situations that no longer serve or support you. Guess what, that also includes your inner critic.

This step is about living bravely before you think you are ready. It is about having the courage to try a new way of being in the world and put your intentions into action. When it comes to saying "yes," it is also about working with what is going on in your life right now. We want to continually make sure that our "yes" aligns with our values and our daily commitments and doesn't derail us in the present while moving closer to our best future self. A quick check-in is to ask yourself, "Does this help me get closer to reintroducing joy into my life?" When you first learn to say yes to the opportunities that are in front of you, joy may not be the first thing you feel, in fact you may even feel a little bit of fear rise up. But when yes and fear meet, it creates the perfect situation for you to Face Everything And Rise. And when you work with your fear, you will be moving closer to the person you want to be and there will be immense joy waiting for you on the other side. You strengthen your courage one yes choice at a time.

Our yes will not always be a success, but it will never be a failure. Within each yes moment we learn how tenacious we can be, we can strengthen our grit and resilience, and we get to expand our creative thinking. All of these are tremendous assets that we then can bring to the next yes opportunity waiting for us. Yes moves us out of our head and into our life.

This is about doing versus thinking, about being in your life versus watching your life from the sidelines. This is about showing up, and then letting go of any expectations and judgments. This step is about exploring your potential and seeing just what you are capable of. You will be amazed at what will unfold. This is about waking up to the fact that your tomorrow is not guaranteed, so what can you say yes to today?

Daily Detox

During this step, we'll focus on a different sort of vocabulary lesson. I want you to look at each word listed here and consider how it might take away or add to your experience of life. Take out your journal and divide your page into four columns. At the top of the first column, write Yes; the second column, No, the third, But, and the fourth, And. Now, fill out each column accordingly:

1. *Yes.* What can you say "yes" to this week that will bring you more joy? For example, in my case, I've starting saying "yes" to new New York experiences, whether with someone else or on my own. This led me to the theater the other night, where I saw *Sunset Boulevard* by myself and had the most incredible time. I've also started saying yes to a new invitation every other week (even when I don't feel on my A game) to attend networking type of events, which is opening so many doors for me.

2. *No.* What can you say "no" to today that is sucking the joy out of you? I'm learning that it's OK to not share my time with everybody, and that I can say no to people who bring me down. If someone depletes your joy, send a polite, but confident "No, thank you" their way.

3. *But.* What are you saying "but" to today? When I'm presenting at conferences, I often get invited to presenter dinners. And my default response: "I would love to, but I'm tired." The "but" in this case was used more as a way out of a situation where I'd have to talk to people I might not know and eat at a restaurant that I might not like. Now, I just say, "I would love to," which has helped me expand relationships all over the world and introduced me to new restaurants in each city I visit. For this detox, I invite you to eliminate the word "but" from your vocabulary, especially if you are using it as an excuse to not try something new or take a small step out of your predictable comfort zone. There will be situations, especially at work, where you may need a deeper explanation. In these instances, see if you can use the word "and" instead of "but." Even if you don't always manage to make the shift, the heightened awareness of the power of your language will be a part of the cleansing process.

4. *And.* What would change, and how would opportunities unfold if you replaced the word "but" with the word "and"? What opportunities would you begin saying yes to if you knew the "and" was a way to help you prepare for your yes? In what areas of your life can you say "and . . . I will ask for help," "and . . . I will try something new," "and . . . I will do the research needed"?

    My sister often comes to visit me and I tend to plan the itinerary, including where we'll be eating. However, on a recent visit she wanted to pick the place we were eating and I hesitantly said OK. The restaurant ended up being fabulous and would go on to become one of my favorites. So now I say to her, "I can't wait for you to come visit *and* discover some of the new places you'd like us to try."

STEP 10

Take Time Out from Social Media

I AM A BIG FAN OF SOCIAL MEDIA, WHICH I USE PROFESSIONALLY TO EXPAND AND EXCHANGE ideas with my network, and socially to stay on top of what's happening in the lives of family, friends, and colleagues from all stages of my life. It has helped me to communicate more broadly yet efficiently, given me useful markers on how to refine my message, and allowed me the pleasure of appreciating the people who have influenced, inspired, and supported me through good times and bad.

Social media also helped me pivot my positioning from one of a fitness expert over to a happiness expert. Suddenly, people were posting happiness (and not fitness) quotes and articles on my page and I was getting booked for speaking gigs on the topic of happiness. Social media platforms were essential to my revealing and rebranding myself as a new type of motivator, as they might have been helpful for you in spreading the word about any of your new endeavors.

Yet, being a social media enthusiast, I am aware of its potential dark side. We have all heard the general concerns about lifestyle changes and productive time loss that the digital media revolution has engendered. The average adult spends three hours a day behind their smartphone (think of what you can accomplish in three hours a day!). And that's for people who didn't grow up with the technology. For millennials, who seem to have absorbed the ways and means of social media into their DNA, the numbers are even more astounding. While the average adult checks their phone 30 times per day, the average millennial checks their phone more than 157 times per day—imagine the lost opportunities for exploration of the immediate world.

Excessive screen time is contributing to increasingly shorter attention spans, which some behavioral scientists now estimate at around eight seconds. Though this science and the implication of the findings are controversial, a quote from a 2016 survey on media consumption sums up an important detail of how life will look like in the future: "The true scarce commodity will be human attention."

In any case, we know that social media is more than just a way of keeping up with news, issues, and networks. It is also more commonly used as a way of keeping up with the Joneses. It is in this way that social media is especially problematic for the perfectionist. Constantly sending out and viewing highly distorted signals of fulfillment, excitement, and other superlative self-congratulations, it triggers all the fears, doubts, obsessions, and illusions that have been constricting the perfectionistic mindset ever tighter.

It is human nature to compare yourself with others. In some cases, comparisons can inspire a healthy impulse to persist and to achieve. Seeing that others are succeeding at something may urge one to find ways to emulate the elements that have worked for them. But we know that the perfectionistic mind doesn't always know when a healthy drive grows wildly out of proportion and becomes an unhealthy fixation.

The comparison game initiated by social media can trip our tendencies to always think that we should have or could have done better, or that our own assets and attributes are lesser than. Social media ruthlessly toys with such perfectionistic notions and impulses. While the perfectionist may have not only kept up but surpassed the Joneses, another person's post might reinforce (falsely) her fear that she hasn't.

Between the ads that are Photoshopped, the images that are filtered, and reality that had its edges blunted, the stream of selfies and "I'm crushing my life" metaphors have the power to undo all the positive work we as perfectionists have done to make peace with ourselves and our life.

When we consider all of this—our lost productivity, our shrinking attention spans, and the caustic effects of comparison—it seems the question should no longer be about whether a time-out from social media would be good for us, but how long this time-out should be. For me, determining the best way to take breaks, and how long they should last, included paying attention to how often I was checking in on the self-curated lives of others and how I was feeling when I shut my screen down.

If you are like I was before I purchased an alarm clock (and before I began charging my phone outside of the bedroom), you are probably on your phone from the moment the alarm goes off, which more than likely is now on your phone. With device in hand as we turn off the buzzer, the option to just "pop on" social media and see what our friends are up to is irresistible. It will not surprise you then, that an hour later you are possibly feeling worse about your life than when you woke up, and your day hasn't even got going yet.

When it comes to social media, or any media that is selling the perfect lie of the perfect life, I am with pastor and author Steven Furtick, who succinctly summed up its effect on the perfectionistic mindset. "The reason we all struggle with insecurity," he said, "is because we compare our behind the scenes with everyone else's highlight reel." We must remind ourselves that what we see on social media is a lovely distortion that has nothing to do with our lives. It may not even have to do much with the lives of those who are posting it.

THE INTOXICATING ALLURE OF OUTWARD APPEARANCES

To regain control of our impulses, we need to stop the flow of images for some interval of time. This practice will save hours—imagine how well you could use the sixty extra days a year (the total annual time, on average, that an American spends on devices). In addition, the headroom you will give yourself to appreciate all that you possess in your life today will be priceless.

On top of the hours lost online, the profound effect that the constant stream of images has on our psyche often goes unnoticed until too late. Humans process images sixty thousand times faster than they do text, and scientists at MIT have discovered that the brain can process images that the eye sees for as little as thirteen milliseconds.

Imagine just how much information we are taking in daily, both consciously and subconsciously—it's no wonder we feel frazzled and riddled with failure. On top of the instant messaging we are consuming, most of it reminding us of how everyone (except us) is living a magnificent and perfect life on social media, we are also bombarded with the stories that traditional media wants us to buy into. Pictures of the latest and greatest products, all selling us on the idea that when you buy their gadget or gizmo you and your life will be perfect.

While we know how much Photoshopping and editing goes into each image, our hearts can't differentiate quite as keenly. These days, the pictures in front of us are digitally enhanced to the point it where it is physically impossible to look like the person gracing the magazine cover, even if we starved ourselves, lived in the gym, and never messed up or had a zit ever again.

Pretty and perfect means you are a success, you are living the American dream, and you have just hit pay dirt when it comes to your happiness. Keeping that in mind it is worth remembering that:

1. Only 4 percent of women around the world consider themselves beautiful
2. Only 11 percent of girls globally are comfortable describing themselves as "beautiful"
3. 72 percent of girls feel tremendous pressure to be beautiful
4. 80 percent of women agree that every woman has something about her that is beautiful but they cannot see their own beauty
5. 54 percent of women globally agree that when it comes to how they look they are their own worst critic

These statistics were collected through the Dove self-esteem project, and they remind us that for most women, beauty equals perfect. Even though I have recovered from most of my perfectionistic habits, I still have to be diligent when it comes to accepting my appearance with grace and gratitude. I encourage you to try and catch yourself, too, in moments when you are comparing and despairing, remind yourself of the gift of your health and being in a body that is able to do everything that you love. And while life is not a bumper sticker, I did laugh when I saw one that read "I will not compare myself to a stranger on the Internet."

While we all understand the lies the perfect images we see every day are selling, our hearts have a hard time separating who we are from whom the media is telling us we should be. For perfectionists, we immediately compare our appearance, both physical and the projection of our lives, to what we see on our screen. This forces us to focus on one small aspect of life—the external representation of ourselves—and with that focus we give it great power, undeservingly so.

In an instant, we forget our accomplishments, core beliefs, values, talents, our personality, and our intellect. And we focus instead on our worth as it's defined only by our appearance. In terms of our sense of self and our self-esteem, this creates a negative impact that will remain in our head and heart, long after the image has scrolled by.

These pictures are the perfect bait to pull us closer into socially prescribed perfectionism, where our drive to be flawless is being driven by the images and messages we see around us. Out of all the maladaptive forms of perfection, including self- and other-oriented, socially prescribed perfection is the most toxic to our health, especially when it comes to our levels of stress, anxiety, and depression.

The challenge for the perfectionist, and also very likely her daughter, who is watching her every move, is that these images and messages are everywhere. Just a few years ago we would need to turn on the television or look at the magazine rack to see perfection. Today, every digital device is reminding us just how imperfect we are, and we will continue to suffer until we choose to reframe how media impacts our lives.

Our world is not going to slow down anytime soon, so it is up to us to prime our minds to be able to observe the images that our friends are posting and find a way to celebrate their happiness. In addition, we need to be vigilant in not comparing and contrasting our life to the stories that traditional media wants us to buy and buy into. I often remind the women I work with that the media sells to our insecurities, but it is time for us to buy into our strengths.

You know what else we lose when we're lost in scrolling, or in those thoughts about what we've seen? Many of life's most precious, fleeting moments. The spectacular firework show, the recently bloomed flowers in your garden, your favorite song played at a live concert, or your children in their latest school play. All watched and experienced from behind your phone. These once-in-a-lifetime moments, while captured on our phone for eternity, will never be captured in our heart in the same way. When we view our life through a screen that is standing between us, and the memories being created—we miss the moment twice.

Being fully present and engaged in our life is one of the keystone principles of this detox, and when we are on social media we are neither present nor engaged. Often used in a mind-numbing fashion to alleviate boredom or to avoid making eye contact with the people right in front of us, we move out of the present. When we move online without intention and lacking our full attention, every selfie and scroll disconnects us from the very part of ourselves that is craving connection.

THE SOCIAL MEDIA STRESS TEST

I am not suggesting that all online social interaction is a negative, but to use technology for the good of our health we need to make sure that we are checking in without checking out. When we are managing our technology wisely, we limit our time on screen and are diligent about how and why we pop onto our social network of choice. We are also mindful of how we feel when online.

For most of us, we don't normally pay attention to how we feel in response to what we see on social media or on beauty sites. But for the sake of this detox, I want you to perform an experiment, a sort of social media stress test. All you have to do is ask yourself a few questions while you're online or shortly after you've logged off. Ask yourself: Do I feel joyful? Am I happier when online or offline? Am I able to enjoy the success of my friends as they share their highlight moments? How is my anxiety level when I am behind a screen and not fully engaged? Also, pay attention to how stressed you feel if you find yourself without your phone or if the battery dies.

As you go through your social media stream, take note of times when you feel wistful, distressed, sad, or angry. Stop and think about what made you feel bad. Look for patterns and try to assess your reaction rationally. Does a picture of a happy family on vacation evoke the images of the ideal you wish you had? Does your friend's thirty-pound weight loss make you feel less happy for her than you would like to admit? Try to think rationally about what is really making you upset, and if it is your perfectionistic mindset, then you know this is a powerful step for you to work through.

We take in so much information through social media but on the flip side we are also responsible for contributing to the noise. As you reflect on what works for your life in terms of intake, how is your output? What do you choose to share and what do you keep to yourself? I had a wake up call about my own "shares" last year.

As you know, I had pivoted my message to happiness. I loved posting positive images and uplifting quotes. What I didn't realize is that I was setting an unrealistic and perfect image for what happiness should look and feel like. I began to get private messages from people asking me how was I able to be so happy all the time? They were comparing their real life to my online happiness and I was making them feel bad! It was a really valuable lesson.

Slowly and authentically I began to share some of the struggles I was having. I didn't do an emotional dump, but I did begin to share my full package. I want my online presence to be as authentic as my offline, and thanks to a few brave souls who reached out to me, I was reminded of a very important lesson: no one connects through perfection.

BREAKING THE ADDICTION

If you are addicted to your screen, know that you are in the majority and it is for a reason. Social networking is engineered to be as habit forming as crack cocaine and to cause a FOMO (Fear of Missing Out). In a recent study by Deloitte, 42 percent of Americans check their phones within five minutes of waking up, and 35 percent of people across the United States check their phones within five minutes of going (or trying to) go to sleep. While the numbers vary slightly depending on which generational group you are focusing on, we all know that our cell phone use is getting out of control. It is time to control the technology before it controls us.

Our cell phone and social media addiction has been blamed on something called the dopamine effect. Dopamine is known as the reward drug, the chemical that is released when we have positive experiences, especially when they are unexpected. Our phones are unpredictable and so those unexpected texts, likes, and positive reinforcement from social media all contribute to a dopamine hit. And while this does contribute to our phone obsession, science is showing that it is not quite as simple as that.

What research does agree on is that checking our cell phone has now become so habitual (and it's not a positive habit) we do it without thinking. Research is offering three main reasons for constantly looking down into our screen: (1) the feeling of pleasure and satisfaction we get from checking our phones, (2) the anxiety of missing something, and (3) the avoidance of social interaction, otherwise known as the shield effect, or boredom.

Facebook is crack for our ego. How many likes, how many shares, and how many "friends" we have all contribute to our status being stroked.

Another feeling that our phones trigger is anxiety. Every time you hear a ding or a beep to let you know you have a new text or message or Facebook alert you receive an adrenaline hit. For our perfectionistic brain, this is not a good thing. Anxiety is on the rise, and as perfectionists we are already wired to feel more anxious than most. At schools, depression is down but anxiety is at an all-time high, which is important to be aware of for your children.

When that adrenaline hits, in addition to taking us at least ten minutes to regain our focus (and if we are trying to excel at work, focus is a key ingredient), our anxiety and stress level goes up. For this very reason I leave my phone on silent unless I am expecting a very important call. While this may not be possible if you have children, what is important to notice is the why and how of when you are behind your screen. Is it for a reason or is it because of habit? Is it researching information or checking out what your ex is doing? Is it sharing images that make you feel happy and you want to spread the love or are you sharing negative tidbits to try and make yourself feel better?

There is not a perfect, one-size-fits-all remedy when it comes to detoxing from social media, but there is a way to check in and do some internal research. It is simply by asking one question of yourself: do I feel more or less joy when I am on my phone? Your answer might not fall completely on one side or the other, but there will be an obvious lean, if you're honest. Consider your response as you work through the instructions of this step.

Daily Detox

1. Pick one day this week to track your social media activities. Do you pick up your smartphone first thing in the morning? Do you go straight to Facebook? Or, are you likely to do so in the evening before bed? Look at your patterns to determine how you can reduce the time spent on devices. Start small, but gradually increase the time-outs. For some, taking one day off a week from social media is just the mental cleanse they need. Some take longer periods off, some just reduce the daily amount. James Hamblin, MD, a senior editor with *The Atlantic*, wrote about an every other day "diet" for social media. In this case, you would "fast" every other day from social media; no Facebook, no Instagram, no Twitter—just you and the everyday activities of your life undocumented and uninterrupted.

   No matter which type of break you decide to take, the respite can work as a reboot to your brain and allow room for real life to lead the way instead of a doctored snapshot captured in selfies. You may find that you like the way this makes you feel more than you "like" the Facebook feedback and decide to limit your exposure to social media for longer periods of time. One simple baby step is to pick a day to keep your phone in your pocket or purse when you're en route to different places. When you're walking or driving somewhere and you have a moment at a red light, or you're a passenger in a car or train, leave your phone alone. Let your eyes wander outward instead; see what you've been missing!

2. Feel free to customize your approach to detoxing from social media, but make an effort to do so—and pay attention to how phone-free periods make you feel. Note, in your journal, if you did something different during your time-out from social media. If you are a fan of Marie Kondo, the international best-selling author whose extreme decluttering strategies have inspired millions around the world to clean out their closets, get rid of used-less, dusty ideas, and spark

joy created a massive movement, you can appreciate the immense benefits of tossing stuff out of your physical and mental space. This is especially true of social media. Think of Instagram. If you are following decorators whose ideas have inspired your renovation project, that's fabulous. If, however, political ideas expressed in the comments of your favorite movie star's stream repeatedly make you anxious, perhaps it is time to unfollow that account. Take the "spark joy" approach to social media: if the images make you feel happy, give you positive and productive ideas to improve anything in your life, then by all means embrace them. If they do the opposite, erase. Unfollow and unfriend mercilessly. You won't miss those accounts and connections. The cost of triggering negativity is always higher than the loss of stimulation that passing images and ideas provide.

Write a Paragraph About Your Proudest Moment

A S PERFECTIONISTS, WE ARE GOOD AT RUMINATING UPON OUR PAST, RECALLING ALL THE events that didn't quite work out as expected. We can pinpoint with precision what exactly held us back from the ideal expectations we so perfectly envisioned, whether these obstructions were people, circumstances, or our own misjudgments.

Nonperfectionists have a slightly easier time identifying and accepting the out-of-our-control variables that impacted events of the past. They are also more effective in allowing themselves to feel hopeful about future outcomes, which for the perfectionist only brings on another set of anxieties of uncertainties to tackle. Being stuck between these two pillars—one of rumination about the past and the other anxiety about the future—makes is particularly difficult for perfectionists to develop awareness about the opportunities of the present and appreciate how far they have already come.

One of my goals in writing this book is that I wanted to share with you the tools for appreciating the past and savoring the present, as these actions will infuse your life with a dose of joy you've been missing. But this challenging perception adjustment is a multistep process, one that requires mindfulness, intense focus, and a positive (as opposed to negative) reassessment. Together, these steps create a new viewpoint of the pivotal moments in your life that have happened, and those that are unfolding now even though you may be less aware of them. Making ourselves more aware requires the presence of positivity, and we've got to do a little work to get her to join the party.

Because our negativity bias is the power player of our mind, I open every Perfection Detox workshop by inviting the audience to take a few minutes to bring to mind three strengths they have. After a few minutes have passed, I then encourage them to take this exercise a step further and write their attributes down. I offer examples ranging from "I am a talented painter" to "I am an empathetic listener," and I tell them that there is no strength too large or too small.

Occasionally the pens begin to move right away, but more often than not, I see most participants in the audience staring at the ceiling, rolling their eyes, or scratching their heads in contemplation and a little confusion. These attendees, who have so much to offer, struggle to recognize *one*, never mind three of their own strengths. Now, had I opened by asking the opposite question, "What are the things in your life you think you are not good at?" I can guarantee you that the pens would hit the paper before I had finished my sentence and that the list would be long and detailed.

In this step, we will exercise a more positive mindset by looking at events (past or current) through a different portal. We will make a deliberate effort to release feelings of shame, regret, sorrow, or anger, those emotions that work to fire up the neural negativity network and zap out the more delicate lace of positive memories or thoughts. Instead, we will assess the situation with a new, bifocal metric. We will only answer two questions:

1. How much have I already accomplished? (Instead of "how far do I still have to go?"—the perfectionist's default position.)
2. How does the past event or current challenge reveal my inner strengths I've neglected to embrace?

Your responses can be uttered internally, if you prefer a mental exercise, or you can grab your journal and get to jotting. Choosing the latter will help prepare you for the main focus of this step—a recollection and a recording of your proudest moment.

RETHINKING PRIDE

One way to steer your thinking in a positive direction is to recall and write a paragraph about your proudest moment. This isn't about recalling in a boastful "I am better than you" sort of way, but rather getting reconnected with the healthy variety of pride that comes from pushing yourself further than you thought you could go, digging deeper than you thought possible, or even helping someone else through a challenging time that they were unable to navigate on their own.

Revisiting these types of moments can remind you of your innate strengths, and of the times you've flexed your courage muscle. When you've pushed your limits and survived a tough time, you have earned the right to feel proud of yourself, and to wear a medal made of resilience and grit. (Can you imagine yourself wearing this medal? Mine is Gratitude and Resilience, invisible to the eyes of others, but nonetheless empowering and, most importantly, a positive reminder that I can do anything.)

Your proudest moment doesn't have to be something that was witnessed by others. In fact, to paraphrase the famous UCLA basketball coach John Wooden, how we act when no one is watching—or at least we think no one is watching—is often the truest representation of our character. You will gain the deepest insight into your potential when you reflect upon those moments you've spent navigating life with no audience and with no expectation of "likes" or "loves" from your social media posts.

I have a complicated relationship with pride. Growing up in England, especially in the north, we were not encouraged to dream big, stand out, or talk about our success. The idea of being prideful was not a positive trait in the British guidebook of life, and this mindset stuck with me for a long time. I still remember my first audition in the United States, on Broadway no less. I was dreaming big, but I knew within three minutes I didn't stand a chance. While I was a decent dancer I certainly wasn't

Broadway caliber, and my singing and acting skills . . . well, let's just say there was a lot of room for improvement.

Upon leaving the audition, I heard one of the girls make a comment to her friend. She simply said, "Wow, I really crushed that audition, I think I've finally got over my nerves and I didn't panic. I think I may get a callback." What I distinctly remember from this event over twenty-five years ago was how triggered I was by the dancer sharing how well she thought she had done. I remember thinking to myself how boastful it was to say something like that out loud.

Over time I have come to understand pride much differently. I see it now as an expression of accomplishment, which we all need to thrive. Best-selling author and psychologist Martin Seligman listed accomplishments as one of the five pillars that are needed to create a flourishing future. (The other four are positive emotion, engagement, relationships, and meaning; PERMA is the acronym that makes this easy to remember.)

Taking this into account, if I were in that same post–Broadway audition situation today, I would have focused on the part about her overcoming her nerves. I know I would have then turned to offer her my congratulations, given her a high five, and shared my own struggles with anxiety.

HOW TO SPOT (AND CELEBRATE) YOUR STRENGTHS

Every time we accomplish something by pushing through or digging deeper, we have drawn upon our innate character strengths. Character strengths are a part of your core being and they cannot be stripped away by perfectionism. As Abraham Lincoln said, "Character is like a tree and reputation like a shadow. The shadow is what we think of it; the tree is the real thing." Because your character strengths are such a part of you, sometimes you forget that you have them. But it is critical that you acknowledge and tap into them daily, especially when things get tough.

According to the VIA Institute on Character, there are twenty-four character strengths that are innate to all humans. If you want to be reminded of what your strengths are and how they stack up, you can visit www.viacharacter.org for a free assessment. In fact, I would encourage you to pause here, take the assessment, and then come back to this page.

They divide these twenty-four strengths into six different categories, and each category can be classified as a virtue. The categories are:

1. *Wisdom and Knowledge:* These consist of our cognitive strengths that we use to gain and use knowledge. They are: Creativity, Curiosity, Judgment, Love of Learning, and Perspective.
2. *Courage:* These relate to our emotional strengths that we draw on in times of external or internal challenges. They are: Bravery, Honesty, Perseverance, and Zest.
3. *Humanity:* These consist of our interpersonal strengths that we use when taking care of or befriending others. They are: Love, Kindness, and Social Intelligence.
4. *Justice:* These consist of our civic strengths that contribute to a healthy community life. They are: Teamwork, Fairness, and Leadership.
5. *Temperance:* The strengths that help us avoid excess. They are: Forgiveness, Humility, Prudence, and Self-Regulation.
6. *Transcendence:* The strengths that forge a connection to the larger universe and provide meaning. They are Appreciation of Beauty and Excellence, Gratitude, Hope, Humor, and Spirituality.

As perfectionists, we have probably failed to give our character strengths proper acknowledgment. We focus on the evidence of how we have not quite met the challenges of the past perfectly and spend our time ruminating on what we could have done better.

I am inviting you to begin to shift your focus, and instead of constantly dwelling on your perceived flaws, begin to enjoy and celebrate your accomplishments. When you allow yourself to savor what you did well, it directs your energy to your strengths that will help you keep your inner critic at bay. When you acknowledge, instead of dismiss your wins and milestones, you start to tap into the vast, barely touched reservoir of your inner power and inner wisdom.

By shifting your focus from all that you think you are "not" to everything that you "are" you expand your lens on the world, and this is the entryway to living bravely. As you sit in the knowledge that you are capable of handling the ups and downs of life, your tolerance for risk will grow and your ability to rebound from failures will become more reflexive.

When you begin to focus on your strengths (not at the exclusion of what you still want to work on) you will find yourself going through the day with more optimism, resilience, curiosity, and joy.

Through my discussions with many perfectionists, I've discovered that they often get stuck around the idea of focusing on their strengths. Their concern is that by focusing on what is going well instead of on what is not going perfectly, they will lose their edge and lose time that should have been spent on fixing, improving, and tweaking.

As a recovering perfectionist, I am no stranger to this sort of logic—we are very good at convincing ourselves that persistence will yield perfection in the end. But here's the truth: it won't, so you might as well look on the bright side of yourself. Now, don't confuse this with a suggestion to simply put on rose-colored glasses and shut out everything but the good. This is an invitation to further establish the new foundation from which you will build your magnificent future. I think you'll be pleasantly surprised to discover that by homing in on your strengths, you will pull up the areas of your life that you feel need improving without it seeming like a punishment.

WHEREVER YOU GO, THERE YOUR STRENGTHS ARE

If you find that you're having a hard time identifying your strengths, I want to encourage you again to take the VIA Survey of Character Strengths (if you haven't already). It is a fantastic way for you to discover all that is working well for you. Scientifically proven, with over four million people already participating, taking this survey and getting your personal results will be like getting your very own courage booster to keep in your back pocket.

Within thirty minutes you will have in your hand a research-based document that lists your character strengths in order. While they will run from strongest to weakest, there may be only a very slight difference between your top and bottom strengths.

Throughout your life, some strengths will remain at the top of the list, for example humor is always in my top five, while others will shift up and down and some will remain stubbornly low. Perseverance is always at the bottom for me and I still struggle to bring zest up the scale. (This is particularly annoying to me as I consider myself quite zesty).

Here is the cool thing, though. When times get challenging or when you find yourself spinning into your perfectionistic negativity, you can always use one of your top five strengths to pull yourself out of the mud and into your best self.

I carry my top five strengths on an index card in my purse. When things feel out of control, I find a quiet space and hold this very tangible reminder in front of me, reading my strengths to myself. The last time I did the assessment my top five strengths were: humor, gratitude, love of learning, kindness, and hope. Not all situations will require the same strength set. If was at odds with my sister, I would pull on gratitude; if I was helping a friend go through a hard time, I would draw on hope; and if I'm struggling with my inner critic I would utilize kindness.

SPOTTING AND CELEBRATING YOUR STRENGTHS IN ACTION

For today's detox, I am going to ask you in a moment to sit and reflect on a time that brings up a sense of pride. I recently did this and here is what popped out from my memory books:

> I feel a great sense of pride when I think about getting through my cancer treatments in 1999. One memory of a doctor's appointment stands out amid many that were all about needle pricks, chemotherapy, and the bald head I grew to cherish. Back then all the medical records were on paper, so on a day where I had two back-to-back appointments at Beth Israel Hospital in New York, I had to manually transfer them from one doctor's office to the office of the next physician I was seeing.
>
> I remember it as a cool but beautiful fall day. I tried to keep my spirits high, even though the stress of two daily doctor appointments challenged this disposition. I asked my friend Howie to come with me for moral support, which is how I ended up with him and another doctor on an elevator.
>
> Just as one should never Google medical symptoms one should never peek into our medical charts on the run. As I glimpsed through the first page of my latest CAT scan I noticed one sentence: "Bowels show signs of constipation."

I looked up at Howie and asked what he thought about the connection between constipation and my cancer diagnosis. Without moment's pause, he turned to me and said, "I always thought you were full of shit and now I have medical proof." I laughed so hard and kept laughing for days after.

Why does this story make me feel so good? Because I realized that it sums up my greatest personal strengths: hope (I told myself repeatedly that I would survive), gratitude (I had my friend Howie by my side), and a sense of humor (being alive is so much more rewarding than being perfect).

In my life's scariest moment, I drew on all three to get myself through it. I may not have done it perfectly, but I did it right. I am, after all, still here. It is also interesting to me that all my top strengths at that time (and still to this day, as they often change every few months) fall under the category of Transcendence.

Daily Detox

- ❖ Write a paragraph about your proudest moment. Can you think of a time when you had to draw on your strengths to make it through challenging times? What did you do? Does thinking about it now still give you a gentle feeling of pride washing over you?
- ❖ If you haven't already, I invite you to take twenty to thirty minutes to complete the VIA character strengths survey. You will feel great afterward. I promise.
- ❖ Place your top five somewhere where you can see them. When your inner critic kicks in, it will serve as a powerful reminder of all that you are versus all that she is telling you that you are not.

STEP 12

Pull the Trigger

IF YOU ARE A PERFECTIONIST, YOU ARE LIKELY TO BE HESITANT TO PULL THE TRIGGER ON actions, decisions, and opportunities. This tendency to postpone can interject itself into just about any part of your life. For example, you might be reluctant to place a phone call, get together with someone you find attractive or intellectually intimidating, pursue your dream job, finish that important assignment or project, and so on.

Of course, you always have a good excuse for putting it off, whether it's that you don't have all the information you need, you want your appearance to look better, you don't have sufficient knowledge or education just yet, your work isn't quite ready for others to view, etc. (We can be wildly creative and convincing when it comes to rationalizing our reticence!)

It's important to explore this habit of procrastination because it's not just a surface issue, and, as it turns out, it's a common and often overlapping one for perfectionists. My conversations with women all over the country have revealed a recurring reason for getting stuck—the lack of a guaranteed perfect and positive outcome.

I know I gave up many opportunities while I waited to be perfect—as a dancer, a woman, a writer, and a teacher. But then I stopped. I realized that if I waited to become a perfect writer I would never write the first paragraph of this book and if I had waited for the flawless presentation rehearsal to happen, I could never muster the courage to be the keynote conference speaker in front of large audiences.

Sometimes you've got to pull the trigger, take a step, big or small, before you think you're ready so that you can move forward. All of us have something that has been on our back burner as we wait for the perfect time to arrive. Guess what? The perfect time to begin is today, in this step. While I won't be asking you to take a huge unrealistic leap into full-blown action, I will be nudging you toward the end of the diving board so that you're ready to take the leap.

PROCRASTINATION NATION

Most of us postpone the inevitable in one form or another. In fact, research by Dr. Piers Steel, a psychologist at the University of Calgary who surveyed over twenty-four thousand people from all over the world, revealed that 95 percent of the participants admitted to procrastinating sometimes, with 25 percent of those confessing to being chronic procrastinators. They might put off paying the bills, doing the laundry, or returning a phone call.

In the dictionary, procrastination is described as putting off something that *should* be done. This covers our bills, our laundry, dishes, projects for work, taxes (OK, maybe those are a must be) . . . but what about our dreams?

Somewhere beyond our list of shoulds and must dos, there lies our list of unrealized dreams. And while we know and understand the consequences of not getting to items on the first list, we don't often think about the consequences of postponing or ignoring the actions we need to take to get to the second.

Yet the negative, insidious consequences are there. When we don't take the leap toward pursuing our dreams, we risk losing our joy, enthusiasm, positivity, and zest for life; we keep our gifts from the world, and we give our inner critic even more ammunition. Sure, we might get safety and predictability, but we sacrifice many of life's most fulfilling emotions and experiences when we don't reach, or at least attempt to reach, our potential.

THE FEAR FACTOR

For perfectionists, the type of procrastination related to our dreams is not about a lack of discipline or willpower, but *fear* disguised as a lack of discipline. This belief has been validated again and again in my workshops. Terry's story is a great example.

I first met Terry at a Perfection Detox workshop last spring. The topic of procrastination came up as were talking through Step 6: Work with Your Imperfections Instead of Pushing Them Away. The participants were sharing their perceived imperfections, and for the most part, the reactions were minimal. Then, Terry shared that one of her imperfections was procrastination, and literally every other participant's hand shot into the air as they said, "Me too!"

Like any other perfectionist, Terry talked about wanting to have all her ducks in a row before she presented something to the world or allowed anyone a glimpse at her effort. She needed to know that the outcome would be a positive one before acting. Terry shared a current procrastination predicament that she was in—she had written an article that she wanted to submit to the *New York Times* in hopes of getting it published, but she could not pull the trigger. She had already spent three months fine-tuning and tweaking the article, but she couldn't bring herself to press send.

At work, Terry was always the one who would complete tasks to get a project in on time. She was also a stand-up comedian and the main caregiver for her mother, both of which require courage, preparation, and follow-through. Yet, when a deeply meaningful personal achievement was on the line, she couldn't seem to draw on these character strengths that she so clearly possessed.

Unchecked, this reluctance to make a move can become status quo. Over time, the perfectionist justifies it as rational and understandable, but every time we postpone taking action on things that we care deeply about, there will be a negative impact. From increasing our stress and anxiety levels to depression, simply putting off tomorrow what we can do today can have serious consequences to our health and happiness.

I asked Terry to look at what might be underlying her procrastination in this case.

After much consideration, Terry shared that it was the fear of being rejected by the *New York Times* that prevented her from pressing send. By waiting to send in her article she could hang out in the gap between thinking and doing. This place felt safe for her, for as long as she remained in the not knowing of what would happen, there would always be the possibility that her article would be accepted.

After working together, Terry was able to move her focus off the outcome and over to the process. She realized that by not pressing send, she was postponing her possibilities for success. If her article was accepted, she had just lost weeks if not months of momentum and likely even additional opportunities. And if it was rejected, Terry had also delayed numerous opportunities for her article to be published in other highly regarded online publications, and who knows what other doors may have opened in the process.

GUESS WHAT? YOU ARE WORTHY

In addition to the fear of failure, another deeply rooted cause to delaying our dreams is that we don't feel worthy of the potential success that is waiting on the other side. As much as we try to appear perfect on the outside, the common thread for many perfectionists is that we never feel perfect enough on the inside to see ourselves as deserving of great success.

We know what to do, we know how to do it, or if we don't, we know we can learn the skills necessary to see it through, but really . . . who am I to believe that my voice, work, book, article, speech, _____ (fill in your dream here) is worth sharing?

Pablo Picasso said, "Only put off until tomorrow what you are willing to die having left undone." When your fear seems too big and the risk of failure too overwhelming, especially when it comes to perfection and pulling the trigger on your dreams, I want you to ask yourself these questions:

- If I only had one year to live, would I be more worried about the risk of failure or more disappointed in the fact that I did not try?
- If I only had six months to live, would I be more worried about the risk of failure or more disappointed in the fact that I did not try?
- If this was my last week on earth, would I be more worried about the risk of failure or more disappointed in the fact that I did not try?

None of us have any guarantees that we will be here next week, never mind next year. Do you want to be in your last few years wondering how your life would have been *if* you had just pulled the trigger? I sincerely doubt that what you have been putting off is a bill, a phone call, or changing a light bulb. My guess is the one thing you have been pushing off to the back burner is something that you care so deeply about, that the possibility of it not working out perfectly seems too much to bear.

PROCRASTINATION OR PERCOLATION? THAT IS THE QUESTION

As much as procrastination isn't healthy, there is a productive form of waiting that I think can be good for you. This process of delaying is something I call percolating. Depending on how old you are, you might remember the percolator, a type of pot used to brew coffee. In this type of brewing, coffee grounds get processed in water as it heats up, then boils, ultimately revealing a potent pot of coffee.

In life, I think there are times when our ideas need to percolate a while before they're ready to be revealed; moments when it is wiser to think things through a little further than pressing the button on going live to the world. This time may be spent beta testing or asking for help to fine-tune a few details; however, there is a large gap between researching and being what my friend and author Susie Moore calls a procrastalearner. I have met so many perfectionists that are also perfect students. There is not a course they have not taken or a book or article they have not read. A procrastalearner is when we use studying to keep us safe, and as a way to avoid sharing our knowledge and our dreams with the world.

If you find yourself constantly pressing pause on your dreams, take some time to sit with yourself and listen quietly. Is it your inner critic telling you that you need to know everything and have everything perfectly lined up to begin? Or is it your inner wisdom advising you to explore one more step before sharing your voice?

SHIFTING YOUR FOCUS FROM THE OUTCOME TO THE OPPORTUNITY

We will never be able to move forward on the things that matter to us when our focus is always on the outcome. If we think of it only as a win or lose, acceptance or rejection, success or failure situation, we will always delay. But what if you stopped worrying about the outcome and began focusing on who you would become by taking the leap?

How we land is not always up to us. It may be a perfect 10, a 6.5, or a crash and burn (never seen that happen yet). But what if we worried less about the landing, and focused our energies on taking the leap? When you shift your focus off the results and onto who you will become by going through the process, you will mobilize your untapped motivation and finally be able to take action.

If you are a perfectionist I can tell you with certainty you are not lazy and you do not lack motivation, but the catalyst behind your motivation up until now has been fear-based. What is it that you are truly afraid of? What would happen if everything did work out? What would happen if 50 percent of it worked out? What if you didn't come close to reaching your initial dream goal, but you started and saw the project through all the way till the end?

When we shift the focus to the progress versus the outcome we open the door to explore a progressive mastery of our life. And with every step forward we strengthen our self-efficacy and self-esteem, and the ability to pull the trigger becomes easier.

We can churn up motivation by taking mini action steps, again and again. Don't wait for the fear to disappear before you start, instead start by slowly chipping away at your fears one action at a time. One day (we just don't know which day), there will be a tipping point. In this moment, you will find yourself taking action and making decisions that move you closer to the things that really matter to you without thinking about it. There will be a realization that the things you used to be afraid of no longer cause anxiety.

This is not to say you will no longer ever have doubts or worries, but they will now be rooted in a knowing that whatever comes your way, you will be ready, willing, and able to take the leap. Will you always succeed? Probably not, but will you always be moving closer to creating joy, living bravely, and creating a life of your dreams.

What if you stopped focusing on what you could lose if it didn't work out and began focusing on all that you would gain by starting and seeing it through? Whatever your "it" is, however big or small, with every "yes and" with every step forward you are expanding your ability to manage uncertainty, you are gaining new insights and discovering new resources, and you will find freedom even in the failures.

Now is the time to begin to move your goals and dreams across the start line. Bring enthusiasm, commitment, and curiosity to each micro step, and whether or not you reach your goal, you will be cultivating a growth mindset that will enable you to live both joyfully and bravely. Begin to look for information versus outcome, for learning versus knowing, and for expansion versus certainty.

One of the greatest illusions that perfection creates is that it will help us soar and shine. Yet our inner critic does not know how to let go in order for us to fly. Procrastination is another win for your inner critic. She thinks by keeping you small and safe you will be able to manage and maintain the illusion of perfection. She is terrified of you taking the leap as this means you no longer need her.

With each mini win and with the support of your friends and fellow recovering perfectionists, you will find that soon the push toward your dreams will have more momentum than the pull toward your fears. Repetition creates mastery, and mastery creates success.

Daily Detox

If it's the weekend or you are feeling especially motivated, feel free to finish this in one session. If you feel anxious about trying to figure this all out perfectly, complete one action step per day for a week. Repeat as needed and then pull the trigger on your dreams.

1. Every dream goal or task can be broken down into smaller starter tasks. To help ensure that you don't get started and then stuck all over again, take out your journal and write down one thing that matters to you, that you have been putting off doing. If you have several, choose the smallest task first.

2. On a separate page write down the things that you normally do to stay busy to avoid taking action to move you closer to this dream goal.

3. Now, write down the recurring thoughts that come up each time you think about starting toward your dream goal.

4. Go back to the page with your goal on it, draw a line down the center of the page. Break your dream goal down into as many bite-size chunks as possible, and on the left side of the page, write down every step that you can think of. Don't worry about the order, but the more micro steps the better.

5. Look at each of these steps and ask yourself if this is a step that you could do yourself, or (if not), if you know someone who would be able to help you, or if you need to do some research. On the right side of the page alongside each step write one of the following: 1. I will do this on (date here) 2. I will ask (friend's name here) on (date here) to help me 3. I will research this by (going to the library, taking a course, etc.) on (date here)

6. Find a trigger buddy, or join the Perfection Detox Facebook community. You will benefit immensely from your new cheerleaders, who just like you are taking the bold step of moving their dreams across the starting line.

7. Every day complete one, just one, mini action that moves you closer to your dreams. One choice, one yes, one small step at a time. Over time your dream goal will become a completed goal. A reminder here to check in with yourself about once a month to make sure your dream goal is still in alignment with your life. Our lives can throw us curveballs both good and bad. Never feel as though you have to see something through to the end if it no longer resonates with you (unless this is a work commitment, etc.)

   Begin, and then even if your dream goal changes, you will have gained much usable research and data that you can apply toward your new dream goal. This information now places you at the half-way mark instead of going all the way back to the starting line. Welcome to the progressive mastery of your life.

STEP 13

Try Again

THE IDEA OF A PLAN OR A GOAL NOT BEING PERFECTLY EXECUTED IS AN EXTREMELY UNSET-tling possibility for a perfectionist to consider. So great is the risk of things not working out just right, and so debilitating this feeling becomes when experienced again and again, that eventually the perfectionist will find excuses to avoid having to take or continue taking action. This is the reason that all unrecovered perfectionists are doomed, at least to some extent, to experience bouts of stagnation and diminished productivity, and they run the risk of giving up before they have given it their all.

If you've lived long enough to reach middle age, you have probably seen examples of this phenomena at play—a talented, hardworking super achiever in the first flush of youth, who plateaus all too soon, and then becomes burned out and steps away from their career, relationship, or potential. No one could see it coming or figure out how or why it happened.

A colleague who regularly attends my workshops shared an example of this scenario with me. As the area fitness manager at one of the top universities in the country, she trains students to become fitness instructors on campus. One of her students was a young man who was "absolutely fantastic," an A+ achiever. Part of the program involved her giving feedback to the students, and this particular gentleman aced pretty much everything, but she shared a single comment with him about one area in which she felt could be even better. Despite all the other accolades that came before this comment, all he saw was the one tiny thing that was not flawless—and he never came back.

We miss a lot when we view something that didn't go perfectly as an absolute failure. I know that for years, I would file away thoughts and memories related to any incidence or experience that involved my making a mistake. I simply could not separate the mistake from my identity; I became the mistake. So, instead of processing, I would tuck away the experience into the deepest, darkest corners of my soul. This made learning from my mistakes impossible, and worse, all but guaranteed that I would make them again.

Even if I did many things well in the process, if I perceived the outcome as a failure, I never stopped to look at and think about it constructively. If I had, I would have been able to apply all that I had learned in the process, create a revised tactic, and more than likely had success on my next iteration. Instead, I repeatedly threw away the baby with the bathwater, as I tossed away the facts with the failures.

This step is a call to stop storing away or suppressing less-than-perfect experiences. Instead, attempt a do-over. For example, imagine enjoying yourself dancing at a wedding or party when suddenly you trip rather embarrassingly. Your reflexive response would be to stop dancing, remove yourself, and shrink into the corner, certain that everyone has seen your footing flub.

Now, when we detox our perfectionistic tendencies, we can practice a different response. In this version, you don't abandon the opportunity to keep experiencing life—you get back onto the dance floor and try to groove with the music as if nothing happened. On the second try you will probably do better. Keep doing it until it doesn't feel as . . . well, wrong or embarrassing. Dance as if no one is watching, because guess what? Most people aren't. In fact, most of them were probably too busy stepping on people's toes, taking selfies, messing up their own moves—and still having a fantastic time.

In this detox, we have learned how to reframe failure and look fear in the eye, but what is it that separates those who have the ability to try, fail, try, and try again from those who try, fail, and give up? It is the ability to be resilient. We practice resilience by shaking off the shame we might experience after any sort of slip up and sauntering back to the dance floor . . . or to the office, the podium, the gym . . . wherever you might have stumbled in the first place.

RESILIENCE TAKES PRACTICE

Life is a series of ebbs and flows, hits and misses, good days and bad. It takes resilience to endure the low points, and to get back up again to keep pursuing the high ones. But it is only when we get up and try again, that we are allowing ourselves to experience the benefits of living in the present and learning in the moment. Author Mary Anne Radmacher wrote, "Courage doesn't always roar. Sometimes courage is the little voice at the end of the day that says I'll try again tomorrow." Even when we miss the bull's eye, we can still garner a mini win from just having made it onto the board and use the knowledge we've gained to give us the confidence we need to be more effective in the immediate and distant future. And this kind of optimism is bound to spill into other areas of our lives.

The author Jonathan Fields has pointed out that there is data in both the kiss and the slap; in other words, that we can learn something from both the pleasure and the pain of an experience. When we get slapped in terms of a rejection or failure, we naturally forget the kiss of how we have expanded and grown by going through the process. The problem with perfectionists is that they don't even know there is a kiss. If we envision or experience anything at all, it is going to be the slap.

We also neglect to see the painful moments as a sign of how much we care. The more we care the more painful the slap. This is not always an easy thing to reconcile, especially right after we get hit. But when we learn that the depth of our fear and anxiety is simply a signal that points us toward what really matters, it can help us reframe how we analyze these emotions and enable us to view them as signs that we are moving closer to our true north. In her book *When Things Fall Apart: Heart Advice for Difficult Times,* Pema Chödrön wrote, "Fear is a natural reaction to moving closer to the truth." Within each disappointment, then, we can find some meaning (and learning), and by focusing on meaning and learning, we can also add a robustness to our resiliency, something that could always use a little reinforcement.

George Bonanno, a clinical psychologist who heads up the Loss, Trauma and Emotion Lab at Columbia University's Teachers College, has been studying resilience for the past twenty-five years. Bonanno found that it is our perception of the event, rather than the event itself, that can make a difference in our results. This is especially true in the mind of a perfectionist.

Think of how quickly your stress and anxiety levels increase during a seemingly challenging moment. These become reflexive reactions that are a result of our feeling as though we have let a secret part of our imperfect self slip out into the world for all to see. From catching a typo in a memo after you hit send, to a flub during a presentation, to noticing our sweater was turned inside out during a job interview, all of these are potential minefields in the mind of a perfectionist. But for the nonperfectionist, these would just be blips on the radar of life. Bonanno reminds us that it is not the actual event that has the power to elevate or deflate us, but it is how we respond to the event that will make the difference in our capacity for resilience.

Just as a positive perception of a situation will build resilience, rumination will drain our tank, especially if we magnify and make up the stories. Bonanno says, "We can create or exaggerate stressors very easily in our own minds. That's the danger of the human condition." This can make the difference between us falling and failing, or falling, failing, and remaining in the game until we have sucked out all the usable data from that particular experience.

THE DAILY DO-OVER

It is one thing to know we need resilience in our life, it is another to know how to tap into it and put it into action, especially during times of adversity and stress. For a perfectionist, the crisis may only be in our mind, but it will hit our nervous system just in the same way a "true" crisis would. The thought that we just failed at something, said something that was not met with approval at work, or made a less-than-perfect entrance into our PTA meeting can spin us into wanting to quit the project, the job, or the meeting and never come back.

Perfectionists try to dodge complications and avoid situations where we may be "found out." This is why that for most of us, the ability to bounce back from a perceived failure can seem overwhelming at times. So instead of trying again we quit. But it is only when we attempt do-over after do-over that we have the opportunity to strengthen our resilience. And it is by showing up, especially when things are not working in our favor, that we learn to live bravely and discover our potential.

The great news is we get about eighteen thousand chances for do-overs each day, where we can strengthen and practice our resilience. The average grownup takes about eighteen thousand breaths during their waking hours, and in between every inhale and exhale we have the power of the pause to create a do-over. Even if you make the effort to embrace a do-over just once a day, you will be strengthening your resilience and over time you'll experience a truly magical transformation.

THE LANGUAGE OF RESILIENCY

In the first phase of this detox, we spent time recognizing, removing, and reframing our negative beliefs. Simply by moving through phase one, you have already increased your resilience level. Now it is just a matter of learning a few additional skills to help you keep moving forward when things become challenging.

Resilience gives us the buoyancy needed to stay afloat when we are in the gap; the gap between where we are and where we want to be, the gap between the knowledge we have and the knowledge we still need to learn; and the gap between living in the uncertainty that changing our relationship with perfection is worth the journey, and the certainty that we are ready for a different way of life.

The challenging thing about resilience is that you can't exactly engineer scenarios that test and strengthen it (you can simulate scenarios, but it's not exactly the same), nor would you probably want to; they have to manifest organically and are often the situations that show up unexpectedly and inconveniently.

Psychologist Edith Grotberg, Ph.D., believed that to cultivate resilience we need to think along the lines of:

1. I Have
2. I Am
3. I Can

I have represents the external support we have around us. *I am* represents the inner strengths, both the ones that we currently possess and the ones that can be developed. And *I can* represents the problem-solving skills that we already have and the skills that we can also acquire.

CULTIVATING RESILIENCE

There are many factors that come into play when we want to improve our ability to stay afloat when things become challenging. One of the key components is cultivating relationships that provide you with role models, assurance, and encouragement. For a perfectionist this can be challenging, as we are comfortable giving advice but are often uncomfortable asking for help. To live bravely, we are going to need to learn how to ask for help, reach out to supportive friends, mentors, and family members, and finally admit that we cannot do all of this alone.

It is time to stop being perfect, and as my mentor Tal Ben-Shahar wisely advises, begin giving ourselves permission to be *perfectly human*. This means relying on yourself as you have always done and also relying on others. This means nurturing yourself and also allowing others to give you support and encouragement. This means allowing yourself to celebrate your strengths and not be sideswiped when you feel weak or are in a place of uncertainty. This means going with life, being with what is, learning from what is working, and also researching what could be done differently when things do not work out as planned.

Thanks to my Perfection Detox podcast, I have been blessed to meet and interview many incredible thought leaders and visionaries. While their stories were all very different, there was one commonality: without fail, those who had a positive role model during their younger years seemed to be able to handle adversity with a sense of hope and a knowing that they would always get through, and over to the other side, of challenging times. Through the positive influences around them, they had learnt how to cultivate resilience at an early age.

For the many of us who may not have had this type of role model, we can learn how to become our own coach and cheerleader. As much as one of our human conditions is the need to be seen by others, it is also important to learn how to see ourselves through the eyes of compassion and acceptance. It is in this space where our resilience can flourish and strengthen. As our resilience deepens, it gives us the capacity to sit and be OK with who we are today *and* still push forward toward to who we want to be tomorrow.

Resilient people are healthier, happier, and are more optimistic as they believe that things can change for the better. The more optimistic we are the greater our level of self-efficacy. Resilient people are willing to ask for help, learn from what did not go well, and try and try again. They have the courage to keep going, even when things are not going perfectly. Resilience does not only show up in the challenging times; even when things are going well, it enables us to cultivate a growth mindset and allows us to focus on the progress versus the perfection.

Daily Detox

A do-over can also be something big, like repairing a relationship or asking for a second chance to do a job right. Both present opportunities for repair and transformation, but I recommend starting small and working your way up to bigger challenges.

1. Take a few moments to write in your journal something that didn't go the way you had hoped and that you wish you could do again. First, write down all the things that did go well and that you would repeat. Then, write down what you would do differently if the situation were to come up again. Maybe you would approach it from a completely different angle or simply make a few minor adjustments.

   If the situation allows you to, and when you feel ready, attempt a do-over. If the event of the past does not allow for a repeat, focus on what you learned from the experience and what you will do differently the next time a similar opportunity comes your way.

2. To help prepare yourself for a do-over and/or to simply strengthen your resilience muscle ask yourself these three questions to help ground your do-over in reality:

- ❖ Who do know that I could ask to help me in preparing for my do-over? (I Have)
- ❖ What went well from my original efforts that I want to bring forward into my do-over? (I Am)
- ❖ What can I do differently next time to make my do-over a success? (I Can)

PART THREE

LIBERATE YOURSELF AND UNLEASH YOUR JOY

STEP 14

Become a Benefit Seeker

IN THIS STEP, I AM INVITING YOU TO BECOME SOMEONE WHO MAKES A DELIBERATE CHOICE EACH day to look for the extraordinary in the seemingly ordinary moments, and to appreciate what may be an opportunity in an otherwise less-than-perfect situation.

Being a benefit seeker will not only elevate your joy, it will also elevate your health and well-being. Many studies have revealed the mental and physical benefits we experience when we choose to focus on the good, especially when it comes to lowering our stress, anxiety, and levels of depression. The World Health Organization recently listed depression as a leading cause of ill health and disability worldwide, with an increase of more than 18 percent between 2005 and 2015. There has never been a more opportune time to become a benefit seeker.

Tal Ben-Shahar—a psychologist, best-selling author, and self-proclaimed recovering perfectionist—puts it succinctly when he says, "Appreciate the good and the good will appreciate." This is a motto that I have adopted into my own program. To appreciate the good, we must first seek the good.

In the beginning, this may feel tough as we have to fight a little against our perfectionistic tendency to spot the problem and not the plus, but we have a super powerful ally in seeking positivity: our brains.

THIS IS YOUR BRAIN ON POSITIVE THOUGHTS

Research in neuroscience, which is the study of how the mammalian brain and the nervous system process information and influence the relationship between thought and behavior, has informed the development of the Perfection Detox Program. I've paid special attention to the area of positive psychology, which, although a relatively new science, has produced some great insights, theories, and evidence-based methodologies that we can use to improve our joy quotient.

One of the most fascinating areas of focus within this field is neuroplasticity. Neuroplasticity refers to our brain's capacity to alter in response to changing thought and action. The science has shown that not only do we have the power to change our thoughts and actions, but that these thoughts and actions can physically alter the pathways in the brain, setting up a revised blueprint for our attitudes and behaviors. What this means is that the adage that thinking positive thoughts can lead to positive behaviors and actions is more than wishful thinking; the scientific evidence suggests that the change occurs on a physiological level in the brain, this of course is in addition to the positive effect we may feel in our hearts.

So, how do we override one tendency to take advantage of another? *We practice.* Positivity, not unlike a muscle, can be trained—and the more you use it, the more you practice, the stronger it becomes. The ability is there for us to tap into the positive thoughts that our brain produces and prime it to focus on what is going well in our lives rather than what is going wrong. We simply have to work on developing new habitual behaviors that fine-tune this ability by conditioning our thoughts to reside in a more positive place.

HOW TO PRACTICE POSITIVITY

The simple act of spending just a few minutes to seek and reflect on three things you are looking forward to will begin to prime your brain to be in the state of benefit seeking. Begin from the moment you wake up. Here's an exercise for tomorrow morning: as you get out of bed, think of three things you are looking forward to during the day, then write them down, and post them somewhere you can see them as a reminder.

Remember that our mind does not like inconsistency between thoughts and external reality and will always try to align them. (Which is why self-sabotage can be a persistent and perplexing problem.) When you start your day from a positive mindset, you will subconsciously direct your actions to align with your intent, and your day is likely to consist of more positive moments than negative.

Heidi, one of the amazing women I had the pleasure of working with recently, shared a story with me about how she became a benefit seeker after an accident that tore her ACL and disabled her for five months. Pain and inconvenience aside, Heidi grew frustrated over her inability to work out properly. But on the day of her surgery, she had an epiphany, which placed her predicament into the right perspective.

As her two kids escorted her to her surgery, a sense of gratitude suddenly overwhelmed her; gratitude for her two children who wanted to help care for her before and after the procedure; gratitude that her excellent surgeon also happened to be a friend who would go the extra mile for her. She was even grateful for the amazing medication, which would put her in a foggy state post-surgery, relieving her pain and setting her on a journey to recovery.

Heidi's story reminds us that at every moment we can make the choice to release the negative and hold on to the positive; that we have the power to seek out and focus on what we stand to gain instead of what we stand to lose.

Today, choose to be a benefit seeker and let your fear of personal flaws and imperfect outcomes move to the backseat where they belong. The habitual choice is to look at the negative, and so don't feel discouraged if at first you don't feel as though you are conquering this step. This upgraded mindset may take time to master, but once you embody the practice your life will flourish.

THE SCIENCE OF HAPPINESS

Everything I'm asking you to do in this detox is grounded in the science of positive psychology (I like to think of this program as providing evidence-based inspiration.)

When it comes to explaining the science behind positive psychology, my favorite book is *The How of Happiness: A New Approach to Getting the Life You Want* by Sonja Lyubomirsky, Ph.D. This book offers easy-to-read research from the science of positive psychology and shows you simple ways to elevate your happiness level.

Research done in 2005 by Lyubomirsky, along with professors Ken Sheldon and David Schkade, revealed (in a now-famous pie chart) that 50 percent of our happiness can be attributed to our genetics, 10 percent is based on circumstances, and a whopping 40 percent is based on our intentional activities. These intentional activities can be broken down into three main components:

1. Finding a sense of meaning and purpose
2. Finding flow (more about this in Step 19)
3. The life choices we make (both large and small)

Lyubomirsky and her associates also determined that when it comes to life choices, one of the most important choices we make daily, even minute to minute, is where we choose to place our attention. Our experience of the world is heavily influenced by where we place our focus, and as writer Ralph Marston reminds us, "Your destiny is to fulfill those things on which you focus most intently. So choose to keep your focus on that which is truly magnificent, beautiful and joyful. Your life is always moving toward something."

Still, there may be times where it will feel challenging just to get out of bed, let alone work on seeking the good. This, my friends, is the human condition and a part of real life. Science sometimes forgets that even proven points about human behavior have to slog through day-to-day living; the statistics have to survive spilled coffee and crappy news, car accidents, and dentist's appointments.

Some critics of positive psychology have suggested that maybe by asking people to only focus on the positive, we are actually making people feel worse. On a bad day, the last thing you want is to feel even more disappointed because you're struggling to see the good. Thankfully, there is a way to be both a realist and an "optimalist," as Tal Ben-Shahar refers to it.

The key is to avoid moving into a space occupied by black or white thinking. If we think that we have to focus on the positive at all costs, even during our darkest times, we are setting ourselves up for failure. But during our ordinary days, when our life is grooving along, we have every capability, should we choose, to be a benefit seeker.

In a recent workshop, I was working through the process how our life opens up when we become benefit seekers, and I could see Lindsay (whom you met earlier in Step 3) starting to drift off. I asked her where her mind had led her, and she answered that she realized how much anxiety and guilt she felt when she was unable to prioritize or focus on the good. She felt bad because she wasn't always able to lead with gratitude, even when seemingly amazing opportunities crossed her path. I was thrilled that she brought this up because this is a universal experience in the cultivation of joy. You will feel it, too—this much I can promise you!

Life ebbs and flows and your emotions will respond accordingly; since you are not a robot, this is completely, 100 percent normal. Your feelings and your dreams (as much as I would like to say otherwise) cannot be completely captured and transformed through a book, a bumper sticker, or an inspirational TED talk. None of this can change the fact that we don't have control over the outside world, a world that will continue to challenge us as long as we continue to walk out the door and interact with it.

I shared a similar sentiment with Lindsay and the other women in my Perfection Detox workshop. As you may recall, Lindsay had recently moved from LA to NYC, and she had admitted that while she knew she should be grateful for the opportunity in front of her, she often had moments of doubt, fear, and anxiety. She had been chosen for the East Coast position in one of the most competitive and prestigious markets in the industry, yet she was struggling to feel only gratefulness and appreciation during the adjustment period. And she was beating herself up for this.

Every time she felt a negative emotion rise up around this new opportunity, she would push it down and reprimand herself. Why couldn't she be perfect, she wondered, even in her own headspace? What Lindsay couldn't see about this experience was that everything about it made her perfect and *perfectly human*. She was awake to her life, aware of all her emotions, the good and the bad.

There will be days where you will find it easy to stay in a state of gratitude, there will be hours when it is a piece of cake to be a benefit seeker, and there will be moments when within the span of a few minutes, you will have moved from benefit seeker to fault finder, over to grateful, around to anxiety, shifted to judgment of your-self, then returned to anxiety, and finally settled back into a state of gratitude.

As a fellow perfectionist, I cannot stress enough the importance of understanding that being a benefit seeker does not always mean that good will show up for you. Please don't label any of your reactions as good or bad, simply allow those moments to move in and out. In addition, when it comes to finding happiness and reclaiming your joy, the question to ask is not, "Am I happy?" but rather, "Could I be happier?"

As you bump around in your emotions, the key is to keep returning over and over to a place that allows you to seek the good. You will bounce back and forth between a positive headspace and the more negative emotions, but the more you make an effort to focus on the good, the easier the practice will become. Eventually your positive focus will become your hangout spot, the place where after much work, your heart, mind, and life will gravitate toward. It will become your new default.

RECOVER, REFRAME, REPEAT

I have been studying, practicing, and speaking about positive psychology for years, but I still need daily tune-ups to stay on course and chart a life of my own design, one that will allow me to maximize my potential. There are days when I have very little problem being a benefit seeker and there are moments when it is all I can do to not cave in, run back into bed, and throw the sheets over my head. I had one of those experiences last week, and it took me a good few hours to shake it off and stop beating myself up for being a "recovering perfectionist fraud."

I had a shoot for an online magazine that I write for called *24Life*. I was scheduled for a video interview and several still photos. The images were going to run in the digital magazine and the video was to run on a loop throughout the 24-Hour Fitness chain of health clubs, meaning that it could be seen by millions of members.

All was going well. Makeup was done, the photographer was amazing, and the director of photography was both encouraging and helpful. I think for any woman growing older with grace and appreciation takes work, and probably the most work of all when we're put under the scrutiny of a camera lens. I know that for me, this is when I feel especially vulnerable.

We had finished the interview portion of things, which I felt went really well, and I headed to the changing room to put on a different outfit for the still photos. In the changing room, there was of course a mirror, one that was lit by rather unflattering lighting, and when I came face-to-face with myself, I was frozen: all I could see were my wrinkles, my age, and the years of living etched on my face. In an instant my heart dropped, my inner critic lit up, and a downward spiral ensued.

I had three minutes to finish changing and adjust my mindset so that I could show up at my best for the remaining pictures. I would be lying if I said this was easy, and I would be remiss if I said I felt 100 percent when I walked back into the other room. What I can honestly tell you is that by using some of the tools that I had learned through the study of positive psychology, I was able to accept what had just happened, adjust my thought process, and show up and give my all to the rest of the day.

That evening when I was at home and reflecting on this experience during the day, I was hit with deep sadness. The sadness was not because I was getting older, but came from me acknowledging that earlier in the day, for a few moments, I had been anything but grateful for my life.

When you become a benefit seeker, it does not mean there will never be future struggles, but it will mean that even in those moments, when you forget to seek the extraordinary in the ordinary, you will refuse to beat yourself up, you will be able to shift your mind back to saying, "I get" to do this instead of, "I have" to do this, and you will be able to rebound and recover more quickly. These moments will also help strengthen your resilience muscle, empower you to build a life of positive focus, and reclaim your joy.

Just as it is easy to practice happiness when you are happy, it is easy to be content with your life when things are going perfectly. Hopefully by this phase of the detox you are gaining glimpses of how your life will unfold as you continue to ease up on yourself and focus on all that you are versus all that you think you are not. As you continue to dismantle and diffuse the pressure to be perfect and resist the lure of the land of doubt, you will be actively staking your claim in the state where goodness can be recognized and celebrated. And this is a "relocation" that will help you create a future that is filled with joy.

Daily Detox

Here are a couple of tips you can follow today and every day to appreciate the good:

1. Place photos of people who love you around your work and play areas and put an image of your beloved place from anywhere on earth on your desktop screen. Both of these actions are positivity primers for your home and work environment. Research by psychologist Ellen Langer has shown the powerful impact our environment has on both our health and happiness. When we create a space that feels warm and calming, the easier it will be to boost our positivity throughout the day.

2. Make a soundtrack for your life by creating a positivity playlist. Put together a group of your favorite feel-good songs that are available to you at the touch of a fingertip. Listening to music is one of the fastest ways to boost your positivity. A 2013 study in *The Journal of Positive Psychology* found that people who listened to upbeat music could improve their moods and boost their happiness in just two weeks.

3. Remember to make a daily list of three things to look forward to in your day. Look for different things throughout your week. This will not only remind you of how much you have in your life to look forward to, but will also help you seek out sources of goodness that you may have overlooked in your past.

STEP 15

Pay Someone a Compliment in Place of a Criticism

WHEN PSYCHOLOGISTS TALK ABOUT THE NEGATIVE ASPECTS OF PERFECTIONISM, THEY break down the condition and its expression into three broad categories. There's (1) the self-oriented perfectionist, (2) the socially-oriented perfectionist, and (3) the other-oriented perfectionist. Even without knowing the full definitions, you might be able to identify which strain of perfection is your nemesis. I could spot mine a mile away: recovered textbook socially-oriented perfectionist, right here.

Of course, it's possible that you see a little of yourself in two or even all three of the categories. A deeper examination of the different types can produce some revelations about the reach of your perfectionistic roots. The steps you've taken thus far might have helped you become more aware of the pain perfection has caused you, but have the effects entangled those you love and even those you work with, too?

In this step, we will explore the varieties of perfectionism, paying particular attention to any projection of unrealistic expectations we may pass onto others through our actions and words that comes with the other-oriented style of perfection. This is not to be confused with an exercise of self-condemnation—it's all about productive exploration. Be sure to keep that in mind. It truly is living bravely to recognize how our own perfectionism affects others.

NOT-SO-TASTY NEAPOLITAN:
THE THREE TYPES OF PERFECTIONISM

See if you can spot yourself in one or more of the variations of perfectionism below:

The **self-oriented perfectionist** is someone who doesn't accept of herself anything less than perfection. This type of perfectionism, depending on how deep it goes, can sometimes be a positive driver. We can use the joy meter to tell us whether or not this type of perfection is working in our favor. For example, did a specific accomplishment leave you feeling fulfilled and full of joy? Or did it inspire you to break out your it's-never-good-enough magnifying glass, which you used to seek out even the smallest of flaws to highlight? There's no joy in that.

The **socially-oriented perfectionist** is the kind of person who presumes that the world she lives in and the people in it expect nothing less than perfection from her. She carries a heavy burden of the perceived criticism (perceived is the key word here) constantly directed her way. Many of us have already experienced how toxic this version is, recognizing the damage that our inner critic and the self-judgments she brings, cause to our health and happiness.

The **other-oriented perfectionist** is a person who expects others to live by the same high standards to which she adheres. This especially vigilant variety of perfectionist sometimes takes her conviction a step further by assuming responsibility for the perfectionistic standards and conformity of others. It isn't an entirely altruistic or conscious effort; her assumption—mostly erroneous—is that the actions of others somehow reflect on her own accomplishment or being. In her mind, the failure of others to meet that bar of perfection is, by extension, her failure.

Of these three expressions of perfectionism, the other-oriented variety is the most insidious and harmful to the perfectionist's relationships. Whether you are a full-blown other-oriented perfectionist or you perhaps just have a mild strain of this virus, or even if you don't recognize yourself in this version at all, when we point the finger and criticize others, we need to remember that there will still be three fingers pointing back toward us.

If you've been on the receiving end of the other-oriented perfectionist you've probably had to suffer through overt or more discreet corrections and criticisms of your words, behaviors, deeds, and efforts. These criticisms might have been coated in the cloak of the "devil's advocate." In this case, the pecking at your work might be justified as being part of the higher cause of helping (but is in fact hindering) you to create the best project, meeting, or whatever else her eagle eyes have landed on.

Nothing you do can ever appease or satisfy a perfectionist whose laser-sharp focus has been trained to spot the most minute of flaws over the most obvious accomplishments. Interestingly, it never occurs to her that the tweaks she offers are neither wanted nor appreciated or particularly helpful. She genuinely believes that her effort is a favor or an act of selfless generosity. The challenge is that as she pokes holes in your work, she always forgets to fill the holes with something positive. With each critique you, your enthusiasm, and your passion sink a little further.

The problem is that the person doling out the corrections and critiques might not, and usually does not, see it this way. It is one thing if the exchange is a one-time occurrence, but in a more intimate or long lasting relationship, it often devolves into a pattern and a habit of which the other-oriented perfectionist is unaware.

The inevitable tension that arises is the reason that so many other-oriented perfectionists have trouble sustaining close relationships. Over time, the other-oriented perfectionist's social circle gets smaller, and she grows more isolated and confused. She almost always feels underappreciated and assumes the people around her are just jealous of her work ethic, which she wears proudly and loudly.

If you can relate to this feeling of underappreciation, you may have some other-oriented tendencies, and you might find yourself feeling a bit uncomfortable, even defensive. And that's OK. Sometimes when a new perspective is brought to our attention, we don't have an Oprah-like Aha! moment, we have an UGH one instead. Yet with a new perspective comes the chance to learn, grow, and change. Whether or not you see yourself as an other-oriented perfectionist, this step will help us all cultivate more compassion, empathy, and collaboration in our relationships.

PUT YOURSELF IN AN "OTHER'S" SHOES

For other-oriented perfectionists, it's important to remember that whatever standard we set for ourselves, it is not beneficial to place this standard on others. Micromanaging and criticism never lead to a more positive relationship, even if the motivation behind it was to improve the outcome in some way. No one wants to be judged, corrected, molded, or perfected by another. The dynamic of constant criticism creates a bad spiral of hurt, withdrawal, and resentment on both sides of the relationship.

The good news is that the downward projection can be halted when the perfectionist learns to stop looking for flaws in others and ceases to offer unwanted commentary or advice. If you are realizing that perhaps you are an other-oriented perfectionist, don't neglect this suggestion: let those around you be themselves, warts and all. Eventually you will come to accept that the attitudes and behaviors of others are not reflections of you. They are reflections of themselves and if you step back, they are probably doing perfectly fine.

If you are looking to build a stronger team, one where your tribe is intrinsically motivated, the only way to create an environment that is flourishing and thriving is through positive interaction and feedback. Pushing your ideas and criticizing those who are not performing in the way you think they "should" be will only lead to reduced self-efficacy and productivity in the long run. Criticism rarely leads to a more perfect outcome. Dr. Martin Paulus, professor of psychiatry at the University of California in San Diego, has studied how the brain reacts when it feels criticized. His work has revealed that when the brain hears a negative word, it processes it as a threat.

When we are criticized, two parts of the brain are triggered: the amygdala and the medial prefrontal cortex. These are areas of our brain that are involved in the fight or flight response. When our fear fires up, areas of the brain that are associated with logic and higher functional thinking become less effective.

Paulus says, "When I engage the brain in criticism, and it is really working hard on that criticism, it can't work on anything else and it becomes all consuming." He goes onto say that "when you engage the brain in very strong negative things, then obviously these negative things become a part of who you are."

So, every time we fire out a negative comment in the hopes that those on the receiving end will be more efficient, productive, and perfect, frankly, the very part of the brain that would be needed to execute the tasks at hand shuts down. And this becomes your mistake, not theirs.

Instead of focusing on bringing others into the orbit of your perfection, concentrate on creating an environment whether at work or at home, where those around you can flourish and thrive. Remember that others aren't going to be grateful for your efforts to improve them, especially if implemented from a place of negativity; they will only begrudge you for making them feel less than (and we all know how lousy that feels).

Anytime we speak less than kindly, we are contributing energy that will only create more doubt, mistrust, and negativity. It is my belief that we are better together, and when we can act, work, and live in harmony with others (even the people who tend to rub us the wrong way), amazing and transformational moments can occur.

Whether or not you view yourself as someone who expects perfection from others, you may subconsciously have silent rules and measurements that you expect others to live up to. When we voice those expectations, especially when we are not choosing our words with care, deep cracks can form in our relationships.

USE YOUR WORDS WISELY

In this step, I'm delivering to you an invitation to be mindful with your words, both the words you use to speak to others and the words you use to speak with yourself. In the book *The Four Agreements*, Don Miguel Ruiz addresses the importance of being impeccable with your word, writing "The word is a force you cannot see, but you can see the manifestation of that force, the expression of the word, which is your own life."

I have worked with many women who struggle with this both at work and with their loved ones. I am often asked, "Where do you draw the line between wanting to help those around you be the best that they can be and expecting or demanding them to excel beyond appropriate measures?"

I believe the most important step is to listen, not just with our ears but our eyes, too. When you interact with others watch carefully and take notice of how they react when you criticize their results versus focus on their efforts.

Some of us already know too well the effect of negative words tossed our way because we were on the receiving end when we ourselves were younger. We were too young then to be able to shield our hearts from the wounds those words caused and are perhaps only now attending to the scars they left.

In a world that often demands perfection, it can be tempting for us to want our team, our partner, and/or our children to rise above the rest and be super successful. But I often wonder what price is being paid because of these expectations. Tension will arise when we demand unrelenting excellence of those around us, and the effects of this unrelenting pressure can be devastating to the relationship.

As I have invited you to do for yourself, perhaps move your eyes off the prize of perfect and over to how those around you show up daily as they strive to be the best that they can be. Help them maintain a growth mindset, one where they can make mistakes, learn through both successes and failures, and flourish in a space knowing that you are not expecting them to be flawless and faultless.

When offering feedback and input, it's important to pay attention to the quality of the words and messages you share throughout your day. This requires intention and full attention; efforts I think we've all let slide a little in modern times. It might take some practice to improve the tone of the messages you deliver to others, but just like with any other skill, you'll get better with it the more often you do it.

This is not to suggest that we ignore the gaps and no longer give input to what could be improved upon. But, when we begin with what is working and then bring in ways that we could improve the things that are not going as well as they could be, it creates a foundation of possibility and positivity versus demands and negativity.

You can start by working on reframing your focus and carefully choosing the words you use. To think before we speak, and to use only words that lift people up instead of tearing them down is an art. To never gossip or speak badly of someone, either through the spoken word, or the words used in emails or in social media; these are practices that everyone should be engaged in. Together, we can all work toward the goal of more productive, thoughtful communication; we'll call it other-oriented positivity.

ASK YOURSELF: WHOSE BUSINESS IS THIS?

If you've recognized other-oriented perfectionist tendencies in yourself and you're working on trying a different approach, you might have noticed that it's difficult to distinguish where your role stops and someone else's begins. Especially during heated moments and in relation to time-sensitive matters, we can sometimes push for perfect and become involved in areas outside of our responsibility.

Byron Katie, author and creator of "The Work," has a simple but effective reminder to help us stay out of other-oriented perfectionism. She has identified what she refers to as "three types of business." They are: My business, Your business, and Whatever-You-Call God's business (she frames God's business as your religious or spiritual beliefs.)

Your business is just that; yours, and this makes it the only business you should be dealing with. A quick exercise, that you can use if you think you may have slipped into micromanaging and criticizing, is to simply pause and ask yourself, "Is this *My* business?"

Sometimes your business puts you in a critic's crosshairs. We all know what it's like to be both a target of criticism and praise.

For me these days, I am better able to deflect and not take personally the few negative comments that cross my path (not easy, but doable). The more I create work that has a message and a viewpoint, the more I realize that not everyone is going to love what I do and how I do it. When I do come across a negative comment, I try to remember what writer and philosopher Elbert Hubbard said, "To avoid criticism (would mean) do nothing, say nothing and be nothing."

YOUR NEW BEST FRIEND: THE DIAMOND RULE

The reason the other-oriented style of perfection is so harmful to our relationships, is because it always comes with criticism that separates us from the people we are working or living with. The words used are tainted with judgment and negativity, which suck out any positive energy from the atmosphere. Whether it is our own inner critic trying to deflect the attention away from our own mistakes, or we truly believe that "others" are just not living up to our standards, as the criticism continues any chance of a flourishing relationship withers.

Perhaps you are familiar with The Golden Rule, speak to others and treat others as you would like to be treated. Then there is The Platinum Rule, speak to others and treat others in the way that they would like to be spoken to. However sometimes we forget The Diamond Rule, which is speak to yourself as you speak to those around you.

This step is about thinking of your words as energy. It is an invitation to detach yourself from other people's work and to stop placing your ideas and ideals upon those around you.

Whether you point fingers, you are the devil's advocate, or perhaps, now and again, you find yourself being a little passive aggressive in your language, we can all elevate the conversations we have with others and with ourselves. The higher the quality of the words we use, the stronger our relationships will be and the more opportunities for growth, potential, possibility, and joy will be created.

Daily Detox

1. In your exchanges with friends, colleagues, and loved ones, notice the moments when your stomach constricts, your throat gets tight or dry, or your heartbeat increases because someone is not performing up to your expectations. Are you able to stay present and calm even if the conversation and situation veers off track? Remember what the author Anne Lamott said, "Expectations are resentments waiting to happen."

2. When thinking about others, catch yourself when you make a negative judgment. Replace that thought immediately with something positive about that person. In fact, for each negative thought, see if you can come up with two things about the person that you like or for which you are grateful. If you have a critique that must be made—if, say, it is work related—make sure you don't do it in a disparaging way. I always suggest when working with teams or family members (especially our children) that we bookend any constructive feedback with a compliment.

3. Before any feedback—or feed forward as I prefer to call it—use the four gates of speech, believed to be based on an ancient Sufi

practice. I find it a very useful tool, both when talking to others and when talking to ourselves. The four gates of speech remind us of the power of our words.

Before bringing attention to a mistake or acknowledging something that needs to be changed, ask yourself these four questions: 1. Is it true? 2. Is it necessary? 3. Is it kind? 4. Is it the right time?

If your feedback can pass these four "gates," then you have my blessing, as even though we are asking that something be changed we are doing it through the lens of compassion, kindness, and empathy.

Move from a Perfectionist to a Passionist

A S SOMEONE WHO HAS SPENT HER FORMATIVE AND PROFESSIONAL YEARS ON STAGE OR in front of an audience, I've been keenly aware of the pressures and anxiety that come with constantly subjecting myself to the standards set by perfection. While a life as a dancer and as a fitness professional did require a certain level of mastery, I never felt as though I mastered anything enough (whatever that even means) and so I was unable to feel proud and joyful, even during the moments of great success.

When I look back I realize that I was really good at what I did, excellent in fact. It pains me to think of how many moments I lost to trying to reach the impossible metric of perfection. I don't want you to lose the time I did by wasting even one more moment living in the shadows of your unfulfilled dreams.

In this step, we are going to work on upgrading your intentions by learning how to focus on excellence and passion rather than the pursuit of perfection. This recalibrated mindset will help you determine appropriate levels of effort and fuel your drive with enthusiasm, while still allowing you to meet and satisfy your ambition.

WHAT IF PERFECTION ISN'T A REQUIREMENT?

Any job, situation, or project we care about comes with a natural dose of nerves, but when we create a win-or-lose scenario with perfection being the benchmark, we are setting the stage for toxic stress and stripping away any opportunity for joy to be experienced. What if I do or say something incorrectly? What if I don't master it flawlessly? What if I fail? This state of high anxiety that comes in partnership with trying to avoid any pitfalls prevents us from discovering our true potential and pursuing our dreams.

As a passionist, you no longer use perfection as the marker of your worth; instead you bring your focus to the task at hand, keep your thoughts in the present by remembering which strengths you can bring to the table, feel comfortable asking for help, and in turn create deep intrinsic motivation by making choices that align with your passion and purpose.

What we often forget is that less-than-perfect results run the gamut from either being critical to mildly consequential to not at all. We neglect to look at life through the facts in front of us and instead often place ridiculously high demands on ourselves. Many times, these impossible-to-meet standards do not even serve the situation we're in.

Of course, there are some situations where being a perfectionist is not only desirable—it is a requirement. If you are a heart surgeon, your margin of error is probably zero; the consequences of being off with your scalpel by less than a millimeter are severe. If that's your profession, your small mistakes and miscalculations can and do have dire consequences. The same is true if you are an astronaut, an airline pilot, or a mother crossing a busy intersection, toddler in tow, on a yellow light. These aren't the kinds of perfection I'm talking about.

For most of us, the demands imposed upon us aren't situational requirements, but instead ones placed on us by our inner critic. When she gets to decide what success means, we lose the joy of exploration, collaboration, and so much more, and leave much of our life untapped for fear of not mastering it perfectly.

THE NEW NOT-SO-NORMAL

One of the most common pain points for perfectionists is that they no longer have a clear sense of what is "normal." What exactly is healthy and realistic goal setting?

What is a normal level of drive and focus? What does a normal body look like? What is a normal process for aging well? What does a normal relationship look like? What is the definition of a super successful, yet normal day?

What nonperfectionists understand about life is that what's normal is *im*perfection. Believing anything different is a set-up for disappointment and failure. In fact, I would say that the day perfection became our normal is the day that the internal barometer by which we distinguish between good, great, or excellent was destroyed. We lost the gauge that could show us what realistic (a.k.a. normal) expectations should look and feel like. Good and great were now viewed as failures because the new normal, the new metric for what we saw as acceptable, was nothing short of flawless.

A perfectionist can't distinguish such nuances because her mindset is so fixed on the outcome. She is further inhibited by the false belief that if she lets go of striving to be perfect in everything, she will no longer be perceived as successful or "good" at anything. That's what my clients tell me. They share their fears that come with being wrapped up in perfection, and their concern that if they let go of perfect their lives may unravel.

The scientific data, however, strongly implies the opposite—that recovering perfectionists become better at jobs when they let go of rigid outcome expectations and concentrate instead on being diligent, productive, and effective.

When they stop trying to be faultless, they not only become more focused workers, they become better friends, parents, and bosses. They work more fluidly and become more authentic in their leadership positions, enjoy more quality time with their children and complete their tasks on time. They work just as hard to attain their goals, but releasing the expectation of perfect outcomes fuels them with joy instead of fear. Outside the suffocating echo chamber of isolation, where they can hear voices other than the one belonging to their inner critic, they find freedom, growth, and opportunities for enriching collaboration. They shift away from the distress of the end goal to the rich rewards inherent in the journey itself.

If we start to transition ourselves into the mindset of a passionist, as is the intention of this step, we can learn to focus on who we already are instead of who we think we should be. This does not mean that you will no longer face disappointment when things do not work out as you had hoped, but you will be disappointed, not devastated. It is time to reclaim a life where we can work hard, coast every now and then, and be able to fail and flourish and find joy along the way.

LET POSSIBILITY BE YOUR DRIVER

In this step, I am not asking you to care less about your work or to lower your standards, instead, I am encouraging you to shift your exclusive focus away from the outcome. This step is about helping you to be your best self and strive for success without sacrificing your sanity, dignity, or joy.

As a performer, I always showed up fully engaged and eager to fulfill audience expectations. What I didn't realize is that because I had a good work ethic and approached all tasks conscientiously, I was already a couple of beats ahead. I wasn't going to falter even if I didn't worry so much. I haven't changed this approach; but I am now able to release my attachment to the outcome. I am now able to roll with the punches better, improvise if something planned didn't follow the plan, and stay in the moment as I invest my creative energies in creating a plan B.

Truthfully, I care more today about my work than I ever did in the past. I would consider what I do now as my calling. I am passionate about my message, and I am able to get better and more proficient as both a speaker and writer, not because of the preventive measures I take not to fail, but because I developed an ability to listen, to receive feedback, and to strengthen my skills by asking for help, without it affecting my self-esteem. I stopped striving to be perfect and concentrated instead on being effective.

Looking back, I can see that I was absolutely driven by fear in the past, but I am now fueled by possibility. Instead of being wary of other people's success, I am inspired by those who have gone further and done better. Being a passionist means still putting in the hours of work and trying to find balance whenever and wherever you can. The biggest difference between this and perfection is that you learn to separate the "you" from what you "do."

Being driven by passion instead of perfection does not mean you will suddenly become a couch potato. In all the workshops, coaching, and speaking I have done around perfectionism, this is the greatest fear that comes up time and time again. The scenarios offered may be different from person to person, but the underlying question remains the same. "If I stop being a perfectionist, will that stop me from being successful?"

I believe that in our hearts, we all know the answer to this question. We will never stop being strivers, but we must, for the sake of our sanity, think hard about what we're willing to sacrifice to an inflexible definition of success. Ask your head, but listen for your heart's responses: what does success look like and feel like to you? Does success have to come with perfection at every level and at any cost? What are you pushing aside to make room for these flawless outcomes? And finally, how would your life expand and broaden if you stopped believing that success is only achieved through perfection and allowed passion and purpose to step into its place?

Inviting passion, purpose, and excellence into our lives lets us see the possibility that exists all around us. We can break free from the restrictive beliefs and boundaries of perfection to make room for real life to step in. Passion softens the rigid edges, blurs the all-or-nothing mentality, and expands our ability to explore both the familiar and the unexpected with courage and resilience.

FOLLOW THE PASSION-BRICKED ROAD

I am inviting you to challenge your ideas around perfection and the road to success, which never follows a straight line. The fixed mindset of the perfectionist steers clear of the unknown, and so she limits her potential before she has even begun, while the growth mindset found in the passionist, views challenges as new opportunities to learn and grow. The perfectionist cannot tolerate the idea of failure and so is always looking ahead with a sense of anxiety, constantly measuring how far she still has to go. The passionist remembers that there are facts in the failures, enabling her to look back, learn from the mistakes, and see just how far she has come.

The passionist works hard and stays up late when needed. She juggles her priorities, as she knows that balance is an illusion. She may have a few sleepless nights and late hours at work or with her children. She has her eye on the new job position that just opened up and is excited and enthusiastic about the challenges and possibilities ahead. She is present for as many of her kids' after-school activities as possible, yet can live in the knowledge that she is being a positive role model for her family on the days she has to be at work later than 4:00 p.m. She is doing what she loves to the best of her abilities at any particular moment in time. Both the passionist and the perfectionist want the same things out of life; the difference is that one is driven by possibility and joy, the other by fear and dread.

I have lived both of these lives and it is my hope that this book and the work you are doing will give you the courage and skills to explore a new way of being. You are still going to achieve great things in this world, but you will no longer have fear in the driver's seat and your inner critic as your coach.

I met Joanna at one of my workshops in NYC. As with most of the women I meet, Joanna seemed self-assured, driven, and confident. For the past four years she had been a successful stylist in NYC and had repeat clientele that had been with her for almost as long as she had been in business. Joanna was about to move her brand online and shared that for the past two weeks she had been paralyzed. Because she needed the online version to be perfect before going live, her new website, which had been ready for the past two weeks, lay dormant.

On a deeper dive, Joanna realized that while she had been busy learning all the things that came with building an online brand and dealing with new challenges that she had never faced before, she had paid zero attention to her existing strengths and proven success. All she could see were her gaps, and the thought of exposing herself and her work in what could possibly be an imperfect website had caused her to spin into a mindset of doubt and fear.

She shared that the pressure of needing her website to be perfect from day one had become debilitating. Every time she reviewed her site she found another small typo or thought of a different way that the pages could be presented. There was always something to be tweaked and adjusted, when would it ever be perfect enough?

In the year it took to build up to her launch, Joanna also realized something else that made this next step even more anxiety provoking, and that was just how important this was to her. Not only had she been percolating this idea in her head for the past year, but she had been carrying this dream in her heart for even longer.

In waiting for everything to be perfect before launching, Joanna had stalled on her potential and her dreams. To build her courage and live bravely, Joanna decided to focus on the positive. She knew that she cared deeply about her customers and brought her heart and soul to all that she does. Joanna made a long list of all that she had already accomplished and understood that for her website to go live, she would need to move perfection out of the driver's seat and put her passion in its place.

On October 1, 2017, Joanna hit live and her website Copper+Rise went out into the world (she used her friends and clients as her trigger buddies). She realized sharing her passion was more important than staying in perfection and decided she would rather risk the possibility of failure than stay stuck in the security of status quo. And to paraphrase Jim Carrey, "You can also fail at what you don't love, so you might as well love what you do."

As we continue to move through the last stretch of this detox, now is the time to look in the mirror and ask yourself, "What dreams and goals have I neglected because there is no guarantee of a perfect win?"

At this point you have already released a lot of the negativity that had been fuel for your perfectionistic tendencies of the past, but is there something that is still anchoring you to the idea that perfect is the only way? Can you unpack the final parts of your belief system that are telling you that perfect equals success? Is there something that is still in your thought process that is silently whispering "anything less than perfect is just not good enough"? If you still hear a soft voice of doubt I invite you to revisit your thoughts behind your behaviors, as this is the last step to detoxing from the limiting beliefs and pain that have been tugging at your soul.

SEEING THE POSITIVE SIDE OF YOUR TRAITS

In her book *Mindfulness*, author and professor of psychology at Harvard, Ellen Langer, writes about research she did with one of her students that will explain why letting go of perfection is often so hard. Langer writes:

> One of my students Loralyn Thompson and I tested the hypothesis that the reason some people have a hard time changing their behavior, no matter how hard they seem to try is that they really value that behavior under a different name. Using a list of negative traits such as rigid, grim, gullible and the like, we asked people to tell us whether they had tried to change this particular quality about themselves and succeeded or failed, or whether the description was irrelevant to them.

Later we had people tell us how much they valued each of a number of traits such as consistency, seriousness, trust, and so one, which were mirror opposites of the negative traits. Our hypothesis was confirmed. People valued specific qualities, that when negatively framed, were the very things they wanted to most change about themselves but had failed to change. Being aware of these dual views should increase our sense of control and success in changing our behavior, if we still feel the behavior is undesirable.

If the thought of letting go of perfection still feels extremely challenging to you, you are not alone. You have been sold the message by people from your past and the media of the present that the perfect life is the successful life. I am not asking you to let go of wanting to be successful, but I am inviting you to change how you think you need to show up to win this success. How can you keep the traits that are working in your favor and dump the ones that are causing you anxiety, stress, and pain?

Here are just a few of the wonderful traits that come along with being a passionist: adventurous, conscientious, dependable, fair, observant, independent, optimistic, intelligent, persistent, capable, charming, precise, confident, dutiful, encouraging, reliable, helpful, humble, imaginative, meticulous, trusting, valiant.

I can tell you that I would be thrilled to be known as someone who lives life in this way and this is someone I would want to work with or be friends with, and someone who I am sure would be a rock star mother, partner, sister, or confidant. Being a passionist still means you are probably going to work harder than most, much harder, but no longer at the expense of your relationships and your joy.

Perfectionists also have their traits, with many coming across as: picky, sullen, finicky, controlling, impulsive, self-centered, unfriendly, and bossy to name a few. Not what we were hoping for. This is certainly not our intention, but what we do and how people view what we do, can often create the opposite reaction to what we were hoping for.

A passionist brings her complete self to all she does, with care and creativity and with precision and purpose. With a joy-filled heart she is able to be in the present moment while working valiantly to create a positive future.

Daily Detox

You now get to embrace all that you already are, instead of focusing on all that you still wish to become. You're on the right track—just keep going!

We'll focus this exercise on a goal or a dream that you've been avoiding or neglecting and view it through the lens of a passionist. Instead of using the SMART acronym that is familiar with goal setting: Specific, Measurable, Attainable, Realistic, Time bound, I am going to ask you seven questions.

These questions are designed to make sure your goals of the past are still in alignment with your values and passion of the present. They will bring your attention to your inner strengths and the resources that are all around you, and by reaching within and asking for help if need be, you will be able to gain the momentum and find the courage to dust off your dreams and move them across the finish line.

To begin, write down your dream goal in as much detail as possible and then answer these seven questions.

1. What do you like best about this goal?

2. When have you been successful in a similar goal or challenge in the past?

3. What strengths can you use to move this goal forward? (Refer to Step 11)

4. What resources do you have to help you move this goal forward?

5. Who can help you with this goal?

6. Which things in your life are helping you move toward this goal?

7. Which things in your life are holding you back from taking action toward your goal?

After you have answered the above, revisit this question from Step 12: If this was my last week on earth, would I be more worried about the risk of failure or more disappointed in the fact that I did not try?

Think of your journey toward your dream goal as marathon versus a sprint. As author and filmmaker Joel A. Barker wrote, "Vision without action is merely a dream. Action without vision just passes time. Vision with action can change the world."

STEP 17

Change Your Relationship with Exercise

ONE OF THE GREATEST HIDEOUTS FOR OUR INNER CRITIC IS EXERCISE. WHILE WE ALL KNOW it is good for our health and great for our brains, exercise will destroy our self-esteem if we make our bodies the canvas upon which our success is painted. I spent over two decades building a strong and vibrant fitness career, but when I really began to look at what women were quietly trying to tell me as they pinched their already tight skin asking me how they could get rid of this or that from their beautiful body, what I saw were women tearing themselves apart as they tried to build their perfect body. Through my own relationship with exercise and the struggles I witnessed from women across the globe, I eventually modified my overall theories on what exercise—which I now prefer to refer to by the broader term of "movement"—means.

A lot of this evolution informed my Moving to Happiness program, which operates from a central question that later found its way into the Perfection Detox: what's your "why" behind your workout? Are you training for a short-term goal or are you training for your best future self? Let me explain.

FINDING MY WAY IN THE FITNESS WORLD

My first job in the fitness industry was in New York in the 1980s, when Jane Fonda sizzled the VHS machines and movies like *Flashdance* and *Perfect*, with Jamie Lee Curtis, defined for us what the ideal, fit female should look like.

If you have no idea what I am talking about, take this moment to rejoice in your youth. Anyway, back then I was a young British expat looking to transition from the uncertainty of being a dancer to what seemed the more professionally reliable job of being a fitness instructor. Culturally, it was a perfect moment for me to put my training, experience, enthusiasm, and knowledge of exercise to good use—which is to help others look and feel better.

They say you have a job, a career, or a calling, and my entry into fitness was certainly closer to being a job. At the time, I lived in Queens, which meant that I had to wake up at 5 a.m. so I could make it on time to open the Manhattan gym at 6:30 a.m., teach a class, and then greet my first set of clients.

I was very high energy, thanks to my excruciating workout regimen of teaching five to six classes a day. I was too busy to eat in between workouts, so most days I chugged down a liquid meal from a plastic bottle while riding the subway into and throughout the city. With sixteen-hour shifts daily all over the island of Manhattan, I was often too tired to eat at the end of the day. This was definitely *work*.

I knew I had reached a certain degree of success when after two years of being in NYC, Reebok offered me a three-year contract to become a sponsored fitness athlete. My job had shifted to a career and I no longer needed to teach classes all over the city to pay the rent. Eventually my work moved me in front of the camera, and along with the increased exposure came the old insecurities of my past.

My on-camera work included television appearances, DVD workouts, and magazine shoots, and I always found such great support from the people "behind the scenes"; no magazine, photographer, or sponsor ever made me feel less than beautiful and right for the job. (Even when I was diagnosed with cancer, lost my hair, and had to wear wigs, no one made me feel inadequate about my appearance, and Reebok never stopped using me, providing a steady paycheck for which I'll always be grateful.) The only person who made me feel that I wasn't just right for the job was *me*—the pressure to be perfect came from within.

My imposter syndrome took over and I couldn't silence the voices from my days of being a dancer. My faulty body image and patterns of thinking placed fuel on the fire of insecurity. Naturally, I was anxious about the future and maintaining the illusion of having it all together, especially when it came to my appearance.

At some point, I began to notice that a day for me would be defined as good or bad depending on the length and quality of my workout routines. If I had managed to get to the gym, pick up the weights and burn the calories, then all was good. If I had to stay home to write proposals, show up for meetings, or fly across the country for an event without a chance to squeeze in the daily workout, then I would silently beat myself up for not getting up at 3:00 a.m. to get to the gym before catching my flight or not going to the gym at 9:00 p.m. after a full day of consulting and creating.

In my mind, all I could focus on was the thought that maybe the workout that I had just missed would be the one that would eventually unravel the career I had worked so hard to establish. The worn-out mental loops of the revered choreographer telling me to drop those few "extra" pounds began their ugly replay, the message once again etching its way into my psyche. From the outside, I looked powerful and in control, but on the inside I couldn't stop feeling that I wasn't thin enough, lean enough, or as fit as a fitness expert should be.

WHAT'S THE "WHY" BEHIND YOUR WORKOUTS?

One of the most important lessons I learned during my own detox from perfectionism is that the feelings of energy and vitality that come with movement, not the caloric burn that we associate with exercise, should be the guiding principle of physical wellness. When we focus on the latter, we can't help but let weight loss and our appearance become the predominant "why" behind our movement. This emphasis on exercise for the sole purpose of changing or maintaining our appearance is a perfectionist trap in waiting, or at the very least, a set-up for disappointment that may feed any negative perfectionistic tendencies.

Why not shift our attention simply to movement itself, not exercise, which makes us more creative, more vital, and triggers the same part of our brains as many antidepressants; it is movement that aligns your body with your mind, elevating both.

How can you tell if your motivation for exercise is healthy? The next time you work out I want you to consider these three questions:

1. Do you look forward to the workout ahead?
2. Does time fly by as you move through the workout?
3. Do you measure your idea of a good workout by how you feel versus the number of calories torched?

If you answered "yes" to all of the above, then you may not need to change your exercise regimen at all. Your motivations are all positive and you are probably benefiting physically and psychologically from the choices you've been making.

But if you find yourself dreading the workout, looking at the clock every ten minutes, or at your wrist so many times you almost get whiplash, then you are probably experiencing less joy and fewer benefits from movement. If you are using exercise solely to lose weight, or drop a dress size, your goals are probably external, solely appearance related, and any success will be short lived.

It's not your fault if you find that you don't experience a lot of joy around working out—the health and fitness industries have all but escorted out the purity of accepting our bodies for where they are today.

As most marketing experts will tell you, the way to get people to buy what you are selling is to tap into their pain point and fears. The fitness industry, which I love and which has been my career for over twenty-five years, has done a lot of great things. We have helped the many who are already fit stay fit, but we have also done a magnificent job of shaming people into exercising.

I think that somewhere along the way, we lost sight that fitness was just a piece of your life-enhancing tool kit, and we made what you look like the definition of success. We missed a wonderful opportunity to share the simple idea that movement is a stepping-stone to your life goals. While your body does need to be ready and healthy (as it is the vehicle that is going to take you on the ride of your life), the success will be in realized dreams. The focus should no longer be whether or not you have a rock hard body, but whether you are healthy enough to rock your life.

LEARNING TO PUT MOVEMENT FIRST

For movement to be sustainable over the course of our lives, it will be the *feeling* that brings us back for more, not the number of reps, or even the calories burned. As part of Moving to Happiness, I invite people to move for any other reason than weight loss and to explore "Why" they work out—a shift that goes hand in hand with the process of detoxing from perfectionism. I see so many people who never get moving because they think they are too unfit to get fit, or are waiting for that perfect time to begin. And as you well know that perfect time never arrives.

To understand fitness through the joy of movement is to understand that we are not created to sit, but instead built to dance, to run, to jump for joy, and to kick fear to the curb. We are designed to stay healthy and vital through vigorous exploration and rituals of caring for our bodies in various ways over time. As author Geneen Roth reminds us: "Your body is the piece of the Universe you've been given." We all need to remember what a privilege it is to have a body that can move, and we should be treating this gift with respect, love, and kindness.

A MOM DISCOVERS HER MOTIVATION

Laurie who you have already met, was one of my first participants in the Perfection Detox workshop in New York City. She had attended my presentation on Moving to Happiness the day earlier and felt so connected to the message that she changed her travel plans to attend the follow-up session the next day.

Normally, when at a fitness conference, Laurie would sign up for spin class after spin class. This particular year, the indoor cycling sessions were limited and so she tried a few lectures that were outside her comfort zone, including my presentations.

On returning home, instead of feeling depleted and drained as she often felt after a weekend away at a fitness conference, Laurie felt recharged and excited, and both her husband and her daughter noticed the difference.

Part of my message had been about thoughtfully considering (or reconsidering) our relationship to exercise, something that led Laurie to make some changes.

She had been filling up her schedule with workout classes, in large part because she wanted to drop some stubborn weight, and she had reached a point of frustration—her workouts were no longer making her happy. So, Laurie made up her mind to mix things up by focusing on at-home workouts instead of going to the gym or a studio.

Part of Laurie's motivation to begin exercising at home is that she might have the chance to include her thirteen-year-old daughter, who was struggling with the typical adolescence-induced self-esteem challenges: she was taller and weighed more than her friends, and so on. Laurie figured that working out with her daughter might give her a chance to instill into her some much-needed confidence in her appearance and potential.

In addition to changing up her routine and joining her daughter, she primed their environment for success. As a family they created large poster boards filled with in-spirational messages (none to do with weight loss) and placed them all around their home gym.

While sticking to these mother-daughter workouts, Laurie never found herself thinking about losing those last few pounds that she hadn't been able to shed when she was focusing on trying to lose weight. But something surprising happened—by changing her exercise routines and location, not only was she able to give her daughter the time and support that she needed, but the few pounds that she had been trying to lose simply fell away.

Laurie doesn't remember her at-home workouts being particularly original or vig-orous; what made the difference is that she infused her workout with meaning other than an arbitrary goal or routines she associated with weight loss. She stopped mov-ing for the sake of numbers and started moving to be better, to feel better, and, in this case, to improve her connection with her daughter. She took her eye off the external scale and tapped instead into the spring of her energy flow, that inner wellness scale that measures vitality and power, not inches and steps. The weight loss was no longer the purpose; yet it was a benefit.

TAKING A LEAP, LITERALLY

In Laurie's case, she changed her "why" behind her workouts, but the truth is so many perfectionists haven't ever considered that movement could allow them to feel free in their body and that they could find flow (more about this in Step 19) in their fitness routine.

I know many who exercise out of the fear of getting older and are fighting the years through sets and reps, others might shy away from exercise altogether because they think this will be just one more area that they are not perfect enough to master. In any of these scenarios, the perfectionist ends up moving for a goal that is rooted in fear or they leave movement out of their life because the fear of failure is too severe to confront.

As someone who used to dance as a living, I was missing the community of dance and the feeling of flow that happened for me when I was learning and mastering a dance routine. I was reminded of this longing each time I walked by Steps on Broadway, one of the most popular dance studios in the country, that's located just a couple of blocks from where I live.

While I've never had a problem taking a dance-inspired class in a gym setting (even after I stopped teaching them), the thought of going back into a dance studio was overwhelming. So, for about a year I would walk by the dance studio and think about taking a class, but I would never go in. Then one day Kimberly, a friend of mine, and I were talking about dance and she also mentioned the desire to go back into class and we decided to make a pact: we would sign up for a beginner adult tap series at Steps.

That first Sunday we were both nervous. While checking in, I mentioned to the girl behind the desk that we both used to be dancers, and she looked up at me and said, "Once a dancer, always a dancer." I smiled, but was still a little unsure. Plus, I was not 100 percent certain that I was wearing was the "perfect" outfit, nor was Kimberly. But you know what? We had a blast.

The class was challenging, yet not so overwhelming that I felt like an idiot. The teacher was funny and treated us like professional dancers and I had a fantastic time dancing alongside my good friend. I realized just how much I would have missed out on had I never put my anxiety and fear out to pasture. The joy and sense of accomplishment I had far outweighed any nerves I had in the beginning.

YOUR GOALS, REDEFINED

I am a big believer in goal setting, as goals create a framework for our lives, but today I would invite you to no longer have any goal around your workouts that's tied to the number on the scale, the number sewn into your jeans, or the numbers on your fitness tracker. The goals that get you up and moving need to be life-enhancing goals, activities that energize you and excite you.

For some, that may be a triathlon or a half marathon, but for many others, a more life-enhancing goal would be traveling to Tuscany next year to take a cooking class, and having the stamina to walk through the hills of Italy with ease. Another goal might be to walk alongside your daughter at her wedding and be able to hit the dance floor for three hours afterward without losing your breath. Perhaps you are getting ready for a new job or a promotion; a goal may be to become more focused, be better able to manage your stress, and be a more compassionate thought leader.

To reach these goals, you may need to get stronger, lose some weight, or become more flexible, however, those are now simply stepping stones to the bigger and more powerful goal of traveling, dancing, leading and living a life filled with moments of joy and meaning.

One way to disconnect from a focus on numbers is to try not getting on a scale for a month. No, you didn't misread this. Do it, Sister! Just put it in the closet. And stop calorie counting, too. Count your blessings instead, and rev up movement, preferably outdoors where you can appreciate being one with nature.

These days, I don't always have time or the desire to go to the gym. When that happens, I take my movement outside. I live in New York City so opportunities abound. But you don't have to be in a great metropolis to find inspiring venues—look for public spaces nearby and engage.

While not all my workouts have changed, the Why behind the workouts has made a complete 180. I no longer care about calories and pay attention to feelings instead. On the day I need to feel grounded, I do yoga. On the day I need more energy I go for a power walk in Central Park. And because I am over fifty, I hit the weights twice a week to keep my bones strong. When I can't do it twice a week, I do it once a week and feel great about it. I no longer beat myself up for not following my exercise agenda perfectly.

This sort of loosening of exercise-related expectations is important for all perfectionists, especially those a bit fanatical about their fitness. To revise your outlook on movement and exercise, start by focusing on a picture bigger than what's measured by numbers.

Remember that while you don't need a rock hard body to rock your life, you do need to move in order to connect with your inner light and your loved ones. And that's where true happiness comes from. When you move, your body and your spirit will soar, and you'll forget all about being perfect and revel in the joy that will pour in!

Daily Detox

For this step, the detox directions are what I call Moving to Happiness Hacks. Find the instructions that speak to you and implement them into your approach to fitness.

1. If you always run five miles every morning, run four instead and spend the extra time on stretching—remember flexibility is as important as strength!

2. If you are new to exercise, get ready to move by standing up. Stand up for five minutes every hour on the hour. One hour at a time. One day at a time. The perfect time to start moving for your health and happiness is today. Sitting is the smoking of our generation and the worst place for your happiness is in a chair. I want to scare the sit out of you and you can put this book down in order to do so. Even if you have worked out today I still invite you to stand more throughout the rest of your day.

3. If you work out every day, I command you to take a day off—your body needs to rest, recover, and reboot. If you are working out seven days a week you are not doing your body any favors. You are setting up the foundation for injury, pain, and ironically, weight gain and muscle loss from possible long- or short-term incapacitation.

4. If your routine always involves high-intensity interval training (HIIT), add some lower intensity workouts into the mix—your body and brain take on high-intensity workouts as stress. Too much and cortisol and adrenaline will be surging through your body, without ever

settling down as they should. Ask yourself, what am I training for? If it is for a long and healthy life, you will need to mix in moderate-intensity workouts throughout your workout regime.

5. Work out with a friend you have not seen in a while. Do something that he or she likes one week, something you like the next week, and then something neither of you have tried the next.

6. When feasible, change work meetings indoors to walking meetings outdoors. (According to his biographer Walter Isaacson, Steve Jobs took his most critical meetings on long walks.) Not only will you get your body moving, your brain will be fired up and ready to create and design. Over time, you will find that your walks and talks will be some of your most productive meetings of the week.

STEP 18

Get Curious

WE ALL HAVE INSIDE US AN AMAZING CAPACITY TO DISCOVER, GROW, BE INSPIRED, AND leave the world a little bit better than when we found it. Yet the perfectionist's world is one that will typically only grow smaller over time. Perfectionism reduces our willingness to play, and because we are so focused on how we appear to others, our ability to explore outside the boundaries of certainty is greatly diminished.

This shrinking effect is a result of the habitual thinking that happens in the perfectionist's mind; the habit being to drive out growth and new experiences due to a fear of missteps and loss of control. The perfectionist chooses predictability over possibility, as the thought of stepping out of her comfort zone and into the unexplored areas of her life feels too overwhelming.

In Step 4, we deconstructed FEAR (False Expectations Appearing Real), and hopefully by now you have a clearer understanding of when and why fear shows up in your life, and how you might work with it instead of against it. In this step, we visit another strategy you can use to the tame the fear and self-judgment that shows up alongside your inner critic. This action step is all about curiosity. As

Irish poet James Stephens once wrote, "Curiosity will conquer fear even more than bravery will."

Now, curiosity is not necessarily the adversary of fear and they are not mutually exclusive—both are imbedded in our psyche and both can be strengthened or weakened depending on where we choose to place our attention. We need curiosity to push boundaries and fear to keep us from falling into an abyss. But in the mind of the perfectionist, fear squashes our inquisitive nature instead of working with it. This detox step will resuscitate our thirst for knowledge and wonder, the inner driver that has been under fear's thumb for too long.

Fear has colored our understanding of curiosity by convincing us that it is an intruder to be approached with caution. Todd Kashdan, professor of psychology at George Mason University and author of the book *Curious?*, writes that "the reason some reject [curiosity] entirely is that they don't feel they can handle or tolerate any of the tension that comes with the unknown." He could have written "perfectionists" in the place of "some" here and the sentence would have been just as accurate!

As far as I'm concerned, this is all just a matter of perspective; we can adjust our perceptions of what it is we can tolerate, and we can be interested about what's on the other side, rather than afraid. Making this shift can bring a sense of play into our lives, make room for new ideas, encourage necessary risks, transform us into better benefit seekers, and allow us to grow into the excitement of new life stages. Our lives and our world will expand as the result.

Curiosity opens our hearts and minds, giving us the opportunity to explore the previously unexamined areas of our life, both the life within, and the life around us. When we are able to create a space that allows us to tap into our imagination, our focus broadens, our ideals become less rigid, and we are able to question our previously set ideas with openness and kindness.

We can also utilize curiosity as we explore our changing relationship with perfectionism. It is hard to hate something that we feel curious about. Imagine how your inner world and dialogue would change, if every conversation and experience were wrapped in curiosity. You would be able to drop the doubt, quiet the judgments, and release the negativity that comes with the fixed perspective that's bound to perfection.

As we shift our attention away from the predictable and into the previously neglected parts of our life, and if we keep a willingness to travel through our lives with the mindset of "what could be," we are able to upgrade our thoughts and actions from those rooted in fear to those driven by an inquisitive mind. Brian Grazer, Oscar-winning producer and author of the book *A Curious Mind*, recommends that we consider curiosity as a super power; we just need the courage to put that power into action.

CURIOSITY OPENS THE DOOR TO POSSIBILITY

Curiosity is the lens through which we can shift the focus from one of judgment to one of appreciative inquiry. Through this viewpoint we can gain powerful insights that will allow us to move safely out of the place of predictability and into a space of opportunity. Many successful leaders acknowledge the importance of bringing curiosity to the table, citing increased competence, confidence, and adaptability as just a few of the benefits.

A 2014 study from the University of California at Davis revealed that when curiosity is stimulated, the brain is primed to learn while also enjoying the process. When our brains become curious they release dopamine, the reward drug; a curious mind then is a happy one, too. This state not only enhances learning, it also improves information retention.

It was curiosity after all that made you pick up this book, so thank you, curiosity! There are many other ways that an open mind can fuel your actions, language, and future. When we are fueled by possibility instead of fear, we are more likely to be intrinsically driven and we are better prepared to stay buoyant during the uncertain times. We will also be more engaged at work, in our relationships, and in our life.

Through the lens of curiosity we are able to seek more of the good, making it easier to be a benefit seeker as it encourages us find more extraordinary moments in the seemingly most ordinary of days.

A JOB, A CAREER, OR A CALLING?

An interest for life, in partnership with our imagination, will give us the tools that we can use to reframe our work from a job into a career and possibly even a calling. This starts by going to work with a beginner's mind and also the having willingness to use your imagination in new ways.

Even if you've been doing the same job for a while, I encourage you to go into work tomorrow with an openness that you may not always have, and challenge yourself to think differently. Look for opportunities that may allow you to ask new questions and meet new people. If a volunteer is needed to engage with another department, be the one to raise your hand. If you'd normally skip out on a team-building session, try checking it out—but be sure to leave your expectations by the door so you give it a fair chance. Be the person who demonstrates a new way, one that is open, alert, and curious. While your workplace environment may not change, your experience will be radically different.

Curiosity is both a character strength and life skill. It keeps us engaged with our family and relevant at work. It is also what allows us to question our ego and check in with our inner compass. If we are to grow and evolve as we age, it is a strength that will enable us to challenge our beliefs of the past and reclaim our values of the present. As I move into my mid-fifties, I am constantly shifting my focus from predictability and over to curiosity. When I look at my future from a place of curiosity and possibility, it gives me the freedom to create a life of my own design instead of waiting for the quality of my life to diminish.

Have you ever noticed that curious people seem to be happier and have more luck both at work and in life? It is not that more luck falls their way, it is because they are looking for what is working instead of the other way around.

In her book *Hunch: Turn Your Everyday Insights into the Next Big Thing*, Bernadette Jiwa writes about the importance of curiosity when it comes to following our intuition and finding the luck. She writes that "The people who have killer hunches are insightful because they intentionally develop three qualities over time: their hunches are born from insights that arise because they are curious, empathetic and imaginative. It's by nurturing these characteristics in ourselves that we become more attuned to opportunities that would otherwise go unnoticed."

IGNITE YOUR IMAGINATION

Albert Einstein once said, "I have no special talents. I am only passionately curious." Think back to when you were young and how you spent hours playing in your imagination and exploring the world through the lens of possibility. We are all born with a mind that is designed to be curious, to think outside the box, and create. But the day someone told you that you were not enough, should know the answer, or told you to stop asking so many questions, was the moment your desire to play, to be creative, and to get curious began to diminish.

The great news is that your imagination and thirst for knowledge are just one thought or question away from being reignited. The challenge is that the world we live in is not set up for us to dive deeply into our own imagination. We have an unending stream of information and ideas coming *at* us from all directions, but the life-changing answers our heart is seeking can only be found from within.

In so many ways, we've become completely uncomfortable with not knowing the answer to questions, no matter what the topic. Don't know an answer? Google it! Rarely do we even give our minds a little mental workout by letting it try to recall something silly, such as what was the name of that favorite song from the eighties? (What was yours? Mine was "Everybody Wants to Rule the World," by Tears for Fears.) This reliance on our smartphones and computers isn't just severely weakening our ability to stay connected to our own memories, it's also damaging our capability to create new ideas and solutions of our own making.

I encourage you to start clearing out the cobwebs and clutter from your underused brain by resisting the urge to Google the answer next time a question comes up (an appropriate question, that is . . . if you're standing in your house with your dog that was just sprayed by a skunk, and you need to know how to de-skunk—Google away! First tip: get out of your house). Give your mind a moment to toss around a query, and just see what comes up, even if it's just additional questions that arise.

A MORE CURIOUS QUESTION

I want you to reflect (avoid rumination, please) on the last project or situation that did not go as smoothly as you had planned. Can you remember the types of questions you had with yourself when this happened? Do any of these sound familiar?

1. How did I let that happen?
2. How did I miss that?

3. Did they notice my mistake?
4. How can I possibly make this work?

These types of questions lead to rumination, worry, self-doubt, additional stress, and anxiety, all of which shut down the parts of your brain that will help you do the next iteration more successfully.

Let's consider the same situation, but I want you to revisit it with questions that come through the lens of expansion and curiosity. Some examples are:

- How could my approach be different?
- Do I need to change my communication skills to make sure we deliver a more satisfying outcome?
- What is it I need to delegate to allow myself the time to focus on the areas that match my strengths?
- Is there something my team is seeing that I am missing?
- What questions should I be asking to get us closer to the results we want?

Curious questions come out of a growth mindset and they will reveal richer, more productive answers. Inside these answers, you might just find the secret sauce to your success; solutions that may have always been there, but you didn't see or couldn't see because of the negative focus that comes with a fixed mindset.

This mental shift can keep you moving forward as you begin to examine the world through the eyes of wonder and imagination. It gives you the capacity to keep going, especially when you feel out of your comfort zone or your insecurity is getting the better of you. With curiosity, we allow ourselves to lean into the uncertainty instead of avoiding it.

When it comes to our future we can craft questions that will help us reconnect with our best self. Below are a few to get you started:

1. What would you most love to do for the rest of your life?
2. What do you most love to talk about?
3. What new ideas or discoveries would you like to be remembered for?

MAKING TIME FOR CURIOSITY?

Curiosity needs to be treated as a gift and as a talent to be nurtured versus just another item on our to-do list. It has been proven to be good for our mind and great for our happiness. It leads into flow (which we talk about in the next step) and allows us to let go of the anxiety that often comes with the rigid thinking of perfectionism.

When we move into a more fluid thought process, we are better able to be in the moment and reap the rewards that come from being mindful. One of the greatest benefits that comes with a higher level of curiosity is the lowered risk of anxiety disorders. In case you need more proof, curiosity is also suspected to play a role in the development of intelligence, wisdom, happiness, and meaning in life and helps us cultivate more satisfying and engaging social relationships. It strengthens our capacity to flourish and thrive in the good times and helps us find new ways up and out of the more challenging times.

Being inquisitive enables us to tap into our intrinsic motivation, develop more attention to an activity, process information more deeply, remember information better, and persist on tasks until goals are met. All wonderful attributes that will help us succeed and soar, yet perfection and fear need to take a back seat for these to lead the way.

According to Kashdan, "Curiosity is different to other ways of being fulfilled in that's about appreciating and seeking out the new. It's about being flexible, recognizing the novelty and the freshness of the familiar. Instead of trying desperately to control our world, as a curious explorer we embrace uncertainty. Instead of trying to be certain and confident, we see our lives as an enjoyable quest to discover, learn and grow. There is nothing to solve, there is no battle waged within us to avoid the tension of being unsure."

This is a powerful way to live as it reminds our perfectionistic brain that there is nothing to fix, nothing to solve, and nothing to perfect. It is about opening up to your life that is simply waiting for you to explore and embrace.

When we become adventurers within our own lives, we spend more time discovering both the familiar and the unknown. We can place a fresh perspective on the more mundane daily tasks and we gain the courage to try new ideas and a different approach (or two) to our life. We dive deeper, stretch our minds further, and get to revisit the past, explore the new, and embrace the future.

In today's detox, I invite you to choose the option that resonates with you. You can come back and revisit this step anytime your imagination needs a curiosity boost.

Daily Detox

❖ Professor Kashdan recommends spending five minutes every day simply being curious. This means choosing an activity and approaching it without preconceptions or interrogations. It means being open-minded to what comes at you and resisting the temptation to look smart, to sound intelligent, to try to disagree with people. My suggestion is to try putting on your curiosity cap at work. How would your day change if you went in with no judgments or expectations and simply asked yourself to reside in a space of curiosity and possibility? Begin with just five minutes. If you like the results slowly expand the time.

❖ Try reading one book on a subject you don't have an opinion on. To determine which one you may want to choose, look at the most recent *New York Times* best-seller list or any of the ten best books of the year lists from reliable sources, such as major national print newspapers and magazines. Ask for a recommendation from an acquaintance you respect but don't always agree with, or simply choose a book that you know your friends will be surprised to see on your bookshelf. If you have time, go to a book reading at a local bookstore and pick up the book from which the guest author is reading. If you prefer to read literary fiction, choose a "guilty pleasure" you've been secretly craving to read—and read it guilt-free!

❖ Watch a TED Talk. There are so many fascinating topics that you can explore. Short in length and full of imaginative and creative ideas that were all sparked by curiosity. Perhaps you will land on one that you would like to explore in more depth.

❖ If you drive a lot or use mass transit every day, subscribe to one new podcast every three months. There are so many wonderful shows, ideas, and topics being discussed every day from all over the world and all points of view. Sign up for a new show, maybe begin with mine, *The Perfection Detox Podcast*, and tune in to hear great conversations with amazing thought leaders and change agents. Every twelve weeks or so, unsubscribe from one and then subscribe to a new show, a new host and dive into a new topic.

❖ Explore a new skill or hobby. It doesn't have to be ongoing, but a one-time class that allows you to expand your curiosity and creativity. Many yoga and fitness studios offer a complimentary, or at least at a discounted price, trial class. Have you always wanted to try pottery or watercolor painting? Give it a go with a child-like mindset—that is, just think of it as fun. Perhaps try a cooking class, one which explores a cuisine you love or teaches you cooking skills 101.

STEP 19

Find Enchantment in the Flow

I N DEFENSE OF PERFECTIONISTS, LET ME JUST SAY THAT WE ARE NOT THE ONLY PERSONALITY TYPE who struggle to make the most of being in the moment. Our brains were designed to mull over the mistakes of the past so we can figure out how to anticipate and evade potential traps in the future. Being more vested in survival than the ability to flourish, the brain's preoccupation with the present is limited, and so we often miss the many opportunities that would allow us to reside in a place of satisfaction and joy.

For most people, the present plays only a supporting role in the otherwise brilliant, innate blueprint that we all carry within us. Reveling in the moment is not a skill at which we are naturally gifted, but it is the missing link between how we would like our future to unfold and how we think we should get there.

The irony is that to build and create a future that is driven by meaning and purpose, we need to be able to reside in the present. Living in the present has always required deliberate thought and effort on our part, and with the advancement of technology, along with the inflated speed at which we are all functioning, the importance of developing this skill is more crucial than ever.

In this step, we are going to learn how to move into being present and to let go of striving for the future. Through these achievements we can create the sensation of a suspension in time; a space in which we are fully absorbed in each and every moment, where our true potential can break out. It is within this space, called flow, that we are finally able to come face-to-face with our best self.

THE FREEDOM ZONE

Hungarian psychologist Mihaly Csikszentmihalyi (pronounced Me-high Cheeks-send-me-high . . . I am never in flow when trying to remember how to pronounce his name!) is the father of flow. If you have ever felt in "the zone" or hit the sweet spot, you have found flow. Flow happens when the activity you are doing and your awareness of the activity merge, melding together to create a liberating sort of hyper-focus where nothing else matters but the current moment. If you are a runner, you might have experienced this sensation as a "runner's high."

We find flow in different areas of our lives. You may find flow in work, in physical activity, or in a hobby, such as cooking. Where you find it depends on your lifestyle, your skills, and your priorities. For example, people who like sports, exercise, or dance often find their flow in the steps and rituals created by these activities, or for the creative types, their sweet spot may be found through painting, pottery, or scrapbooking.

Due to the hyper-alert state that a perfectionist's brain is often in, many times we miss the magic and momentum that is available to us through this super state. The forces of fear and anxiety about not getting it right inevitably get in the way. Without realizing it, each time we try to dodge a bullet we are also missing the opportunity to meet our best self.

When I was performing, my anxious brain regularly hijacked my ability to fall into the flow state. My mind was always so focused on not making a mistake and trying to always appear perfect, that there was no way for me to remain in the moment. This type of focus proved to be counterproductive and ultimately erected a roadblock between me and my best work. Stuck in my own internal commentary, controlled by rapid-fire judgment, I was unable to get out of my own head and let my true potential come to life.

For perfectionists, there is always something *other* (usually grounded in fear or anxiety) that's grabbing our attention: a thought, a to-do list, or another note from our inner critic that pulls us out of the moment and back into the madness. In our minds, there is never enough time to get everything done perfectly. But what if I told you that it is when you lose track of time that your excellence can finally emerge?

The suspended, timeless quality of flow makes it a place where we can find freedom from perfection, while still creating our best future. It is the space where you drop all the self-judgments that continually pull you out of the present moment and tap into your courage instead. No longer hearing the noise that comes with the rumination and worry from your inner critic, you will be moved into a place of positive hyper-focus, concentration, and awareness.

Flow is where you get to notice the insights that will enable you to create the excellent work, project, or outcome that you have been longing to achieve. In this state, you get to witness the sensation of a life devoid of perfectionism, the place in your body and mind where you are finally able to find peace.

It turns out that the type of peace that's engineered through flow can also be beneficial to your overall performance in many different areas of your life. At least according to author and researcher Steven Kotler, who created the Flow Genome Project along with high-performance expert Jamie Wheal. Kotler was recently featured in a *Huffington Post* article in which he shared that "studies show that altered states [including flow] boost motivation and creativity nearly 400 percent, while cutting learning times in half."

Kotler went on to say, "When doing what we most love [it] transforms us into the best possible version of ourselves and that version hints at even greater future possibilities, the urge to explore those possibilities becomes feverish compulsion. Intrinsic motivation goes through the roof. Thus, flow becomes an alternative path to mastery, sans the misery." For a perfectionist, flow is a reliable way to attain the reward that always eludes her—satisfaction in the effort and enjoyment along the way.

When you stop searching and become absorbed in the present, you get to feel both excited about, and engaged in the life you are living. Perfection has no impact on your success, and no longer standing on the sidelines, you are all in and ready to meet your best future self.

THIS IS YOUR BRAIN ON FLOW

There is a place in our brains where tension resides, created by the collision of signals coming from the stoic frontal cortex (the voice of reason) and our hyper-alert amygdala (anxiety's impulsive warrior princesses residing in another part of the brain). These signals can clash as they work to guide our thought and decision-making processes.

When our brain moves into flow, the tension dissipates as the part of our brain responsible for self-monitoring becomes quiet, and you know who lives there? Our inner critic. When your brain is in flow, she has no air to breathe, and no power over you, your process, or your potential. As the part of your brain that loves to be the judge and jury of your decisions loses its power, your inner critic finally shuts up (and not a moment too soon). This is one of the many reasons that finding flow is so vital for perfectionists.

In 2008, neuroscientist Charles Limb did a study examining the brains of jazz musicians while they were improvising and in a state of flow. MRIs revealed that the part of the brain that is responsible for self-monitoring was deactivated in the musicians as they just played without pressure.

This "deactivation" can allow us perfectionists to move into a more fluid state where there's no room for negativity to interfere, and where we can experience a sense of enjoyment. Accessing this state can also allow us to meet our courage, creativity, spontaneity, and freedom; things that our perfectionistic tendencies often prevent us from experiencing.

While you are in a state of flow there is no room for doubt to exist. Your fears and anxiety are forced out of the driver's seat and into the background of your consciousness where they should remain, deflated. It is in this state that you are primed to experience your optimal potential.

Not only did Mihaly Csikszentmihalyi recognize and name the concept of flow, he has studied the impact of flow upon our lives, and researched specifically how the flow state relates to our experience of enjoyment and success, and how it may assist us in accessing our potential.

He has found that enjoyment, which leads to intrinsic motivation and in turn greater success, has eight components. When one or more of these are present, it is likely that we will access flow. These are:

1. Complete concentration on the task at hand
2. Clarity of goals with reward in mind and immediate feedback
3. Transformation of time (it feels like time is speeding up or slowing down)
4. The experience is intrinsically rewarding; it has an end to itself
5. It feels effortless and comes with a sense of ease
6. There is a balance between challenge and skill
7. Actions and awareness are merged
8. There is a feeling of control over the task

When I read this list, I think *I can't get to flow fast enough!* Flow is also a success catalyst, which for a perfectionist is a double win. You finally get to enjoy the journey while also improving your results—what a concept. The question is of course: how do we get to flow?

FINDING OUR FLOW

Flow is not always easy to describe, but we know immediately when we have experienced it. These are our power moments, the moments where magic happens and when we are in our zone. Those times when you look up at the clock and three hours have passed, but to you it feels like it's been ten minutes.

Being able to drop into flow whenever and wherever we want takes a lot of practice, and even the top performers in the world can have difficulty finding their zone. Researcher Owen Schaffer (who worked under Csikszentmihalyi) created a flow condition checklist. I find this a useful guide to help us tap into our super state more frequently. When we can set up our environment to maximize the following criteria, it will help prime our surroundings to enable us to find our flow:

1. You know what to do
2. You know how to do it

3. You know how well you are doing
4. You know where to go (if navigation is involved)
5. There are high perceived challenges
6. You have high perceived skills
7. You are free from distractions

Flow is the place where we stop seeking and start being. We find contentment by being absorbed in whatever we are doing and it is here that our creativity and imagination can be unlocked and released. This is when our mind becomes the perfect vessel for imaginative ideas and solutions to unfold. Flow offers the perfectionist a vacation from her normal state of worry and anxiety, a respite from her own mind.

I find that one of the quickest ways for me to drop into flow these days is to take a camera (not my smartphone) with me on my travels. Whether in nature, in the middle of NYC, or in a foreign city, the moment I decide I want to slow down and drop into flow, I simply focus on seeing the world through the lens of a camera. Before I know it, hours will have passed without my knowledge. I am totally in the moment, seeking new things to photograph, and any worries or anxieties in my life disappear.

You may find your flow is running, hiking, over dinner and in deep conversation with good friends, being with your pets, or babysitting your grandbabies. Others have found it in the kitchen cooking, or when they knit, draw, or play a musical instrument. All of these allow you to be in the moment and of the moment.

Another favorite way for me to drop into flow is through listening to music. When I am watching any competitive sport, many of the athletes will be wearing their headphones right up until they are called for their race or event. When I was doing research for this chapter, I reached out to my good friend and phenomenal athlete, Dara Torres. Dara has competed in five Olympic Games, is a twelve-time medalist, and in 2008 became the oldest female swimmer to compete in the Beijing Olympics. She took home three silver medals as in the 50-meter freestyle race she heartbreakingly missed the gold by 1/100th of a second. She was also known to always wear a huge pair of headphones right up until her races.

I would always watch her compete and often she would text me the day of the race to let me know how she was doing. On TV, you could see her walk into the pool area with the biggest smile on her face, big headphones on her ears. You just knew that she was rocking her favorite tunes to help her get into the right mindset. When I asked Dara about these intense pre-race moments, she shared with me that music played a huge role in getting into her zone and entering her peak state before stepping onto the blocks.

Music is a powerful resource to help us bypass our inner critic. Whether or not you ever compete in the Olympics, I recommend you create a power playlist for the days you need an extra boost.

Using the examples above, consider this: You can't think too much about the mistake you just made at a meeting or the upcoming school project when you are focusing on your new watercolor painting. Similarly, you can't think about the punctuation problems in your kid's college application form if you are writing poetry or taking a photograph. You can't rehash a recent argument with your sister, boss, or neighbor if you are designing the pattern on the sweater you are sewing. Etc.

For flow to occur, the activity you are doing should keep you fully engaged and be suited to the skill set of the task at hand. (That is the reason this Detox step is not to be confused with Step 16: Get Curious, which calls for teaching or engaging yourself into something new to expand your horizons, although there may be some overlap of the two).

Being in a flow state is not about adding intense, transformative tension into your life. Too much of a challenge and you will become anxious and drop out of flow; not enough healthy stimulus to hold your attention, and you will become bored and fall out of flow. Find just the right amount of challenge, and it will be for you the ecstatic satisfaction that Goldilocks found among the possessions of The Three Bears. You will find that golden moment, and it will be just right for you to drop into the delightful space of the here and now.

There are also opportunities for flow to be found at work. You can help ready the environment by focusing on tasks where you can utilize your character strengths (Step 11) and spend more time using your natural skills in the work that you do. This may mean delegating, which for a perfectionist can feel extremely threatening. But when we can spend more time working in our strengths, and in turn allow others to work on projects that highlight their skill sets, a rich and rewarding work environment will be created, one that is buoyed by flow, creativity, and collaboration.

GIVE YOURSELF THE GIFT OF FLOW

Just remember that wherever your flow may be, you can't allow yourself to think about it as an indulgence. (That will trigger feelings of guilt and shame, the perfectionist's master saboteurs.) Think of flow as a necessity and an investment at being your best, rather than an instrument for orchestrating perfect outcomes.

We should all be in this state at least two hours per week as it is active recovery for our mind. Don't panic at the thought of having to do it all at once, although once you begin to find flow you may get hooked. This time can be chunked down into shorter periods of time and sprinkled throughout your week. Begin to think how and where you can weave more moments of flow into your day.

To discover where you find flow, reflect to the last time you felt time disappear. During this activity your worries slipped away and you felt both energized and focused. Recall that moment in your life and then ask yourself these questions:

1. Where was I?
2. Who was with me?
3. What was I doing?
4. How did I feel?

Finding the answer will help you find the Goldilocks bliss point we all carry within. Once you identify the components of your past flow experiences, try to bring these pieces together again and more often in your present and future.

Daily Detox

This week, work on introducing more flow moments into your day. Don't feel as though you must jump in with two hours the first week, but slowly build up the amount of "flow time"; think of it as play time for your mind.

1. Exercise—if you are not a newbie to exercise, consider changing up your routine. It needs to be something you enjoy and not a workout where you force yourself into the room. It also would be best if it was something where you're not focused in any way on your caloric burn or weight loss—you won't get into a flow state when you're preoccupied with these types of goals.

   This is where my idea of Moving to Happiness can help you; aim to move for pleasure and enjoyment, without the need to evaluate your performance. That being said, if you love to run, are energized by the thought of competition, and are intrinsically motivated to jump out of bed and get to the gym, it is likely that you already find some flow through fitness.

   If you want to increase your experience of flow or if you feel that you've hit a stagnation point, why not try a new instructor who uses different music or even a new workout entirely? Or instead of going to the gym, perhaps you could enjoy a walk outside in nature, or go to a dance studio or boxing gym?

2. Take time to sit and listen to some of your favorite music. When you put your music on, really listen. Notice the changes in rhythm, the different instruments, the vocals and the style. Listen to it actively and with curiosity. When listened to intently, music can bring you into a state of flow.

3. Draw, sketch, or paint. Pull out those watercolors or buy an adult coloring book.

4. If you have a pet, spend more time with your furry friend. Play with them, brush them, and really be in the moment with them. Furry flow at its best.

5. Family flow. Flow can be found when we spend quality time with our family. Create one evening a week when all electronics are to be put away. Break out the games and spend a couple of hours reconnecting with your loved ones.

Make Peace with the Mirror

I F THERE IS A DAILY REMINDER OF OUR IMPERFECTIONS, NONE IS AS GLARING AS THE MIRROR. Whatever your age, feeling fully at ease with your appearance can be tricky, even trickier for those of us who already struggle to reconcile who we are with who we believe we should be.

The mirror reminds us of our mistakes, our flaws, and everything that is one degree from perfect. It also toys with our heads, hearts, and logic. When we focus on our wrinkles, acne, or extra pounds, the emphasis gains energy and eventually becomes just another piece of ammunition to use against ourselves. On the rare occasion that we look into a mirror and think, "I don't look too bad," we automatically give credit to the good lighting. Crazy, sad, and self-esteem draining at its finest.

Our inner critic relishes in the moments of ruthless appearance analysis; every time we look in the mirror and see ourselves as less than perfectly human, she chimes in with comparisons that will help strengthen the case. When she says to you, "Psssst . . . look at the woman over there—she's much prettier, younger, and thinner than you," you can't resist. She's only confirming your fears, and the flaws you see each day in the mirror. This is a soul-destroying cycle. It's time to break free from it.

In this step, we are going to learn how to stop ruminating on our physique and our appearance. From trying to be the perfect size, to wearing the perfect outfit, to not wanting to stand out, to being afraid of not fitting in, ridding ourselves of the stream of appearance-related self-criticism is an essential part of this detox.

MORE THAN JUST PARTS OF A WHOLE

I know few women who can look into a mirror and view themselves in their entirety. Most of us see only bits and pieces, vulnerable parts that we can separate from our wholeness and easily attack. Achilles had his heel, I have my neck, and you likely have your own "part" or "trouble zone" that draws your attention. And where your attention goes, your energy flows. As our eyes lock onto the parts of ourselves we loathe, our hearts will follow and our inner light will begin to dim.

It has taken me decades to make friends with the mirror. I wouldn't say we are best buddies, but at least I am no longer at war with her. The crazy thing is, when I was at my physical best I was so detached from my inner light I couldn't appreciate any of it.

I also think that whatever we don't like about ourselves is typically what we worship in others. And this is why self-acceptance is often seen as the key to shedding so many destructive emotions including envy. For many years, I would look at people's legs as I had what they call English Man's disease. It was the one certain thing I inherited from my father: terrible veins. By the age of twenty-five, I had the varicose veins of an old man, and I felt such shame about the appearance of my legs that I always wore jeans, pants, or long dresses, even during the summer.

Eventually, I did have surgery on my legs as the pain was becoming unbearable and my "new" legs—minus the veins—were super fun to have. Although, this fun was short-lived since the veins returned just a few short years later. I came to a decision that I would stop trying to keep up with perfect legs. If the pain once again became unbearable, I would look at new options, but outside of that I decided to accept and appreciate my legs, veins and all.

There was also a time where I regularly went in for Botox injections. It began with me feeling as though I needed to be perfect to be on camera, and it moved into me trying to fight my age. I syringed literally thousands of dollars into my face.

That was until I had a treatment, or rather parts of my face, go sideways. The doctor had decided to inject some Botox under my chin and another bit that went a little too close to my right eye. As a result, the right side of my mouth was paralyzed and my right eye was droopy. So, every time I smiled all I could focus on was my droopy eye and my crooked smile—it was terrifying! The thing I loved most about my face—my smile—was no longer mine.

After three months of not looking like myself, I decided that I would rather have more wrinkles on a face that I recognized, than a smooth face that didn't belong to me. I like to say that I used to inject thousands of dollars into my face and now I inject that money into my business.

I have no judgment whatsoever about the use of Botox or fillers or any type of cosmetic or corrective surgery, but I think it's important that we do some work on ourselves before we do that kind of work. My experiences revealed powerful truths—that pain-free legs that could jump, run, tap, jazz, and high kick were plenty sexy, and that I *did* love certain attributes of myself, even though I didn't realize it until they were changed.

Even if I might make the same choices if I could do it all over again, I would wish for a greater degree of kindness in my internal messages during those times. I remember thinking that my legs were going to be the ruin of my fitness career, or that the wrinkles emerging around my eyes and mouth would be the end of my time on camera, and I could not have been harder on myself about these factors that were beyond my control. Of course, as a perfectionist, control was irrelevant—the flaws in my appearance were my fault, and they reflected gross failures on my part.

I consider this the first part of my plea to work on making peace with what you see in the mirror, including those parts that irk you the most. The mirror reflects back to us what we think and not what we actually see. The moment you make a negative judgment about what you see when you meet your reflection, you have just bought into the lies doled out by your inner critic and split yourself into pieces. And pieces aren't peace, but reflective of the "broken" way we sometimes look at ourselves.

BROKEN EYES

Annie, whom you met in Step 8 (and who also happens to be a good friend of mine), calls this seeing ourselves through "broken eyes." When I first met Annie, she was in a recovery group for overeating and on the upside of recovering from bulimia. Thirty years later, she no longer struggles with food and body image, yet still struggles to fully embrace herself in the mirror due to the imperfections associated with aging.

I think "broken eyes" is a perfect description for how we look at ourselves.

Women of all shapes and sizes look in the mirror and pause, then they move in a little closer and zero in on their faults and flaws. Without fail they then begin to pick themselves apart.

When was the last time you looked in the mirror and smiled at yourself? When was the last time you caught a glimpse of your reflection in a shop window and gave yourself a high five? When is the last time you looked at yourself without broken eyes?

How about today is the day we begin to see not only ourselves through the eyes of wisdom and kindness, but also every other woman who crosses our path? Whether we know them or they are strangers, whether we stop to talk or we walk on by, quietly we offer a gaze to them that says, you are beautiful, you are strong, and I am honored to call you my warrior sister. We are all at war with our inner critic, and as we finally begin to treat ourselves as we would treat those we love, together we can rise up and finally shut those inner demons down.

THE TRUTH ABOUT STORIES

The problem with mirrors and how we view other women is that it is only a reflection of the stories we are telling ourselves. As we see the women all around us, what goes unseen is the truth of their life and the beautiful battle scars. Both of which are hidden under the lies of perfection.

If you were to meet Jennifer, you would see what I saw the first time she came to a Perfection Detox workshop. A vivacious and super successful trainer who was rising through the ranks at warp speed. She had a body that any woman would crave and physically she could do anything with ease and grace (or so I thought).

What I and those who knew Jennifer could not see was that underneath her "perfect" body was a thick layer of toxic shame and sadness. We were not witness to the fact that Jennifer and her husband had been trying to conceive for the past five years. That seemingly perfect body was not cooperating in creating the perfect family. Every time someone asked Jennifer when she was going to have kids she would brush it aside, saying that she and her husband were focusing on their business. As Jennifer explained to me, what made matters worse was that by being in an industry where everyone viewed her as the perfect specimen, she was terrified to share her struggles as she would no longer be seen as the perfect leader. The gap between the Jennifer people saw and the truth of how she was living built up to chronic levels of stress and anxiety. So much so that she realized for the sake of her health she could no longer go on living the perfect lie.

Jennifer decided to share her struggles with those around her. The support and love was overwhelming and many women (including her sister-in-law) also shared their own battles with fertility. By being brave and sharing her truth, Jennifer not only began the process of healing, but also made so many women that she worked with feel less alone in their struggles. She continues to thrive in her career and is slowly finding her way back to happiness as she makes peace with her new normal.

As warrior sisters let's always remember that within every woman is a shadow story or two. These are the stories that float in the gap between who we are and who we pretend to be. Together we can bring these shadows to the surface and shine a light on them to begin the healing process. This begins by cultivating conversations that are rooted in truth, empathy, and compassion.

MAYBE WE SHOULD JUST BREAK OUR MIRRORS INSTEAD?

If I could tell you to never look in a mirror again, I would. But that is not realistic and also not that helpful. Mirrors are everywhere, in the restrooms, in our homes, in the gym, in the office and also thinly disguised as shop windows. And their reflections send many a woman into a stream of negative self-talk.

If you pay attention, it's easy to spot the inner critic and the less-than-ideal reactions to our own reflections. I see it in other women at the gym, and in the faces of those out shopping. I can sense the inner conversations that are occurring, moment by moment and glance by glance. The self-talk of hating our bodies, the dislike of the effects of aging, and the soft worship of wishing we could live up to the images of the women we see in magazines and on TV.

But these mirrors tell so little of our stories, and leave so much out about who we are beyond our reflections. Mirrors can only show us the skin in which we live, and it neglects to show us the depth of our kindness, empathy, compassion, and courage; our strength, resiliency, humor, or any of the countless other offerings of character we may have. If we remain more connected to the reflection, rather than what lies beneath, we will never realize our full potential, or get to know our whole selves.

For us to take the final leap into living bravely we have to accept all of ourselves, no matter what our size, age, or wrinkle level. Taking the leap means learning to exercise our luxury of choice (we sometimes forget that we have this, and I'm here to remind you!). I get to choose if I see my wrinkles as a liability or an asset, my age as something to hide or promote, and my body as something to appreciate or despise. You get to choose whether you treat yourself with love and appreciation or fear (of aging) and loathing (of your looks).

I'm not saying it's easy to make this choice; in fact, it can be extremely challenging because it goes against everything society has taught you and everything perfectionism tells us that we should be.

To find the power you need to choose acceptance; you've got to tap into the brave place that resides deep within, the part of you that does not buy into what you are told and sold every day—the lie that we need to be beautiful, young, and wrinkle free to be worthy of having a life of our dreams. The part of you that has been untouched and is unscathed by the outside world, and is immune to your inner critic. In this place, you will meet the authentic you. The beautiful person you already were before any role model or media told you that you needed to be different than who you are.

GET REAL: THE REACH OF YOUR REFLECTION

The way we see ourselves in the mirror and the messages we send back to our hearts influence how we treat ourselves but also can determine how much we engage in life as it's happening around us. Each time we choose to look at ourselves through broken eyes, our self-esteem weakens, our life becomes smaller, and we lose another opportunity to live bravely.

From avoiding being in a group photo, to turning down a potential date, to not going on a vacation with friends. From always wearing black, to never trying a new way of dressing, one that highlights your curves instead of diminishing them. From buying a dress size too big so that it does not hug your body, to not going to an event because you feel fat. All of these choices begin with the glance in the mirror. Instead of groaning next time you look at your reflection, try giving yourself a wink and see how it makes you feel.

I am not perfect when it comes to my relationship with the mirror but during my extraordinary of ordinary days, I see all of me and I am proud of the work that I am contributing to the world. I appreciate my body and train to feel strong, energetic, and focused. I still struggle in the moments that I am being photographed for a magazine or for a video shoot, but I recognize this is a battle and often use the associated article or interview as an opportunity to share my struggles and hopefully make others feel less alone.

I no longer turn down opportunities to network, speak, or be on camera simply because I feel a certain way. I say "yes" even on the days I am seeing myself through my broken eyes. I say yes to my life and no to the voice of my inner critic. She is often there on the sidelines waiting to pounce, but I catch her sooner rather than later and use the strategies in this book to shut her down before she can trample on my dreams.

When you learn to live bravely you give other women permission to do the same. By showing up and feeling complete, even on the days when things are not going to plan, you become a guiding light for others who may have lost their way.

In her book *Love 2.0: How Our Supreme Emotion Affects Everything We Feel, Think, Do and Become*, Barbara L. Fredrickson wrote about how the resurgence of our own self-acceptance can be a vital part in helping us connect better with others: "When your reserves of self-love are low, you can scarcely meet the gaze of others, seeing yourself as either beneath or above them. A chasm forms between you and others that slashes your odds of forging true connections. Yet when you practice and bank self-love, you become rich with emotional reserves. You're more able to recognize sources of goodness in others, to see and fulfill others' yearnings to connect, no matter their circumstances."

For us to truly be benefit seekers, brave-living individuals, we have to first seek the truth of who we are, and then fall in love with the person whose reflection we see in the mirror. Every time we look at ourselves through open eyes and with a compassionate heart, we create more space to live bravely and help others do the same.

SEE THE BEAUTIFUL TRUTH OF WHO YOU ARE

I want to invite you to begin to look in the mirror from the eyes of your best friend and live each and every day bravely and with joy. A brave woman will show up fully, in her light, and without dimming the light of others. She thrives around other women, celebrates their wins, and shares in the burden of their losses. She does not define her worth by the price tag on her clothes or by the number on the scale. She measures her worth in friendships, moments of presence and striving to be the best that she can be without sacrificing her joy. As brave women, we want success and to do our best, but it is not until we finally make peace with the mirror and all it represents that we will be able to step fully into our bliss.

The mirror reflects back to us what we think and not what we actually see. Think you are too old to be beautiful and that is your truth. Think you are too unfit to go for your dreams and that is your truth. Believe you are powerful, brave, strong, kind, and ready to put work into your dreams, and that will be your truth, one that will lead you into your magnificent future.

Daily Detox

1. Commit a week to not looking in mirrors once you have gotten ready for work. If at the gym, do your strength workout facing away from the mirror, or lower your gaze to the floor. (This will also add a balance challenge into your fitness routine.) Notice the difference in how you feel.

2. Find a role model in your own life for how to live well as you age. If you have a vision of what kind of person you want to be in your later-in-life years, you are more likely to take the steps to get there.

3. Edit your drawer of age-defying products—I'm not saying you have to get rid of them, just review what you already have. Buy the best product you can afford, but don't stock up on more items than you

need just to feel like you are battling the process. We will never win a "war" against aging; we must instead aim to practice productive and proactive self-care so we can be our best (not perfect!) selves as our age increases.

You can tell how well I am doing this by how many neck creams are sitting on my bathroom counter. Just like Nora Ephron, my neck has been my Achilles' heel in aging, but I remember that I have a choice to become better with age and not bitter about aging, and that I will indeed be crafting a well-lived life, and at fifty-four, as I write this book, I still have (hopefully) a lot of living to do.

4. Make a shopping list—what do you need to make you *feel* younger, rather than *look* younger?

5. Remember that it is a privilege to get older, not everyone has that luxury.

6. If you catch yourself glancing in the mirror and getting into it with your self-esteem, revisit your mantra from Step 2: "I am enough," "Be here now," or "I refuse to beat myself up."

7. To move out of the little "I," find a cause to commit to outside of yourself. Something that will benefit others in the long term and make you feel like you've contributed something to a mission larger than yourself. The cause doesn't have to be the kind that aims to change the world; but it should be meaningful, at least to you.

Let Go of Your Past and Create Your Magnificent Future

WELCOME TO YOUR MAGNIFICENT FUTURE, ONE WHERE YOU FEEL FULFILLED, EXCITED, and joyous. This is a time in your life where your days are filled with satisfaction, positive experiences, and reassuring reflection as you focus on your accomplishments. This way of living is right at your fingertips, and perhaps as we enter the last step of the detox, you have already begun to experience these kinds of moments.

Maybe your anxiety is downgrading as you begin to feel more comfortable in your skin. Perhaps the new awareness of your negativity triggers is enabling you to create a more productive and joy-producing environment. Most importantly, you are realizing that you are not alone, and you have a new understanding that we are all much more alike in our struggle to appear perfect than we are different.

In fact, as you read this, there is a new tribe forming around you. Wise women of all ages who, just like you who are committing to a different way of living, one where they use joy as their metric for success. Women who are finally facing themselves head on and loving what they see.

This final step is where you begin to paint outside the lines of your past while coming back to honoring the core of who you are. Staying true to your values and connected to what makes you thrive and flourish. This is the moment to say goodbye to the shame, guilt, and regrets and hello to your joy-filled future.

In workshops, I've found that this moment in the detox tends to represent an interesting departure point. For many participants, while they share with me that they are already beginning to tread more lightly and joyfully through their days, I sometimes hear of a new pain point; the pain of realizing how many opportunities and moments have been lost to the dreaded disease of perfectionism.

To this, I say: whatever your age, and however long you have been dragging around this burden, now is the moment to let it all go. Let go of your regrets about lost time and release the thoughts of how you would have done "it" differently.

Unwittingly, the very thing we thought was going to fuel our magnificent future ended up dragging us further and further away from all we had to offer. But you did the best you could with what you knew at the time. And now you know better. This is the moment you ease up and forgive yourself. Your life is waiting for you but it is only when you release your regrets of the past that your magnificent future will have room to enter.

FORGIVENESS EQUALS A WAY FORWARD

Forgiveness has always felt a little elusive to me. What does it really mean, and how can we forgive ourselves when we realize just how much damage we allowed our perfectionism to create?

In Step 5, I mentioned something a therapist shared with me many years ago, and I think it is worth repeating as we enter the last step of this detox. As you read the next sentence I want you to think about forgiveness in terms of forgiving yourself. While we all know the importance of forgiving others, rarely do we think about tending to our own self and heart in the same way. Here's what she said:

"Forgiveness is not letting people off the hook (including yourself) for doing unforgivable things, but it is about unhooking yourself from the negative actions of the past so they do not affect your positive future."

Forgiveness does not require us to do anything, rather it invites us to release the things that are no longer serving us. This includes beating yourself up for the moments, days, months, and perhaps years that you may feel were lost in the existential Bermuda Triangle of perfectionism.

On the other side of forgiveness is responsibility. Perfectionism has already eaten up too many of your memories, and when we take on responsibility for creating our forward-thinking future, we allow for our lives to flourish in a sustainable way. We will be able to weather the ups and downs of real life, versus the ups and downs that we used to create in our mind.

ANCHORING TO THE PRESENT
TO FLOAT IN THE FUTURE

To remain buoyant and at our optimal potential, we must take the reins of responsibility and create actions that anchor ourselves in the power of today. We know by now that the present moment is the only place where we will be able to efficiently catch any perfectionistic outliers, turn them around, and release them. Perfection may try to take root at any time; even when we have pulled out the negative weeds, there may be a few seeds left that could sprout in the future.

This is not an invitation to begin shoring yourself up for what *may* happen, but rather an invitation to settle into yourself, knowing that you have done the work and will be ready and able to address your inner critic and any of her false stories that may arise in the future.

To stay ahead of your inner critic, it will be necessary to prime your heart and mind so that you remain your own best friend. Thinking of yourself as a friend whose company you enjoy is a powerful perfectionism repellant. This is why it's important for you to continue to nurture your relationship with yourself, and to ensure that it's one that consists of conversations that are grounded in compassion and understanding. A friendship of this type is one that can elicit calm instead of anxiety, joy not worry, and hope instead of dread. And as you continue to strengthen this friendship, your ability to accept even imperfect moments will improve.

STAYING CONNECTED TO SMALL CHOICES

Another way to fortify the friendship with yourself is to continue to focus on the quality of your micro decisions. The seemingly small choices we make inform our moments, which in turn affect our days and our lives. We can choose to be a benefit seeker, not a fault finder; to look forward to our days with anticipation and look back on them with appreciation; to lead with kindness, not criticism.

These aren't quick fixes, but long-term practices for you to keep in mind. In other words, you have to keep doing the work for it to work. Here are some other ways to help you keep pesky perfectionistic tendencies at bay:

1. Revisit this book every so often, and repeat the steps and strategies that resonate with you most. You may want to also consider returning to the ones that made you the most uncomfortable, or that you skipped entirely. These steps might represent the places where you will find the greatest opportunities for growth.

2. I will also be offering numerous other tools that I hope you'll take advantage of. This includes podcasts, morning reminders, research updates, and additional resources, all of which can be found online at ThePerfectionDetox.com. Since there's a certain degree of "technology" needed to access these tools, I do want to remind you to always manage your technology so that it does not manage you. I too will be mindful of this and protect and respect your time and attention accordingly.

YOUR JOURNEY TO JOY

Just as the road to success is never a straight line, neither is the journey to your powerful and positive future. I wish I could say that as this chapter comes to a close, your inner critic will be smashed inside the cover when you close it, but she won't. She may show up in a new outfit, with a new accent (I hear she loves to travel to France), and maybe even in the disguise of someone you have yet to meet.

What I can tell you is that if you work this work, she will no longer have any power over you. You will no longer make decisions based on her desires versus your dreams, and you will be able to quiet her voice as soon as she raises her hand, accent and all.

This is a time to look forward to your tomorrows with a sense of wonder and possibility. A time to feel excited about the life that is waiting to unfold for you. A life that without question always has your best interest at heart. The road will not always be smooth, and my guess is that there will be a few bumps in front of you, but that is life. Just like time, life has no opinions about the choices you make, it only asks that you are awake for the ride.

YOUR GPS FOR LIVING BRAVELY

I am inviting you to begin living with what you know for sure. Do not fill in the blanks with your beliefs as no matter how far you have come, your default will still be to draw from the negative. You know your strengths, you know your values, and we know for certain that there is much outside of our control. As much as you can, reside in the present, as this is where your power, bravery, and joy will unfold. The more presence you bring to your life, the more days will overflow with joy, creating a new path forward fueled by possibility and action.

The more you trust in yourself, the more you will thrive. The more you thrive, the more your life will flourish. The more you flourish, the better able you will be to help those around you do the same. Live as you would want your loved ones to live. When we are more joyful, our family will be more joyful. Joy-filled families create joy-filled communities, and together we cause a ripple effect to elevate the joy in the world in which we live.

REMOVE THE BURDEN, REPLACE WITH THE BLOSSOM

As we let go of the past we make room for our potential to blossom, and for some of you this may feel like very uncertain territory. Perhaps a life without perfection feels a little untethered, and this is why it is important to visualize your positive future. There is much science that shows the benefits of taking time to imagine our best future self. Act "as if" and one day "it will be so."

Laura A. King, professor of psychology at the University of Missouri, conducted a study in 2001 where she invited participants to spend twenty minutes over four consecutive days imagining in detail their ideal future and best future selves. They were invited to think in great detail about how it would look, where they would be, what would they be doing, and how would they feel. After just eighty minutes, all of the participants reported sustained elevated levels of optimism and well-being.

There have been many subsequent variations of this exercise, and I am inviting you to take it one step further by adding into the exercise a visualization of a life free from perfectionism. Begin by choosing a time frame six months to three years in the future, and then:

1. Imagine that all had gone well and nothing had gotten in your way.
2. You had detoxed from perfectionism and were comfortable with making mistakes and asking for help when needed.
3. Imagine in detail where you worked hard and all the steps you took to get to this place. Think of this as your dream goal coming to fruition. It needs to be realistic and attainable, even if it is with a lot of work and effort.
4. Now, write this down in present tense as though it had already happened. Be sure to include as much detail as possible: where you are, who you are with, what you are doing, and how you are feeling.

This can be done as part of your detox and I would invite you to come back and repeat this exercise anytime you feel unsure of your future desires. In addition to helping you remember what is important to you, it will remind you of the steps you need to take as you continue the journey from the amazing person you are today into your best future self.

There are many strategies (most that you have already explored) that will help you step up bravely into an unpredictable and flourishing life. As this part of our journey together comes to a close, I want you to keep coming back to the simple question: "What can I do today to bring more joy into my life?"

THE STRONGEST FOUNDATION OF ALL IS LOVE

To cultivate a sustainable approach that lays the groundwork for your best future self, you will want to broaden and build your future from a foundation of love and joy versus doubt and fear. The more micro moments of love and joy you can build into your day, the more opportunities will step forth for you.

Barbara L. Fredrickson, Ph.D., whom I mentioned in the previous chapter and who is a thought leader in the world of positive psychology, writes, "What I've found is that even though you experience positive emotions as exquisitely subtle and brief, such moments can ignite powerful forces of growth in your life. They do this first by opening you up: Your outlook quite literally expands as you come under the influence of any of several positive emotions. Put simply, you see more as your vision widens, you see the bigger picture. With this momentarily broadened, more encompassing mind-set, you become more flexible, attuned to others, creative and wise."

Fredrickson goes on to write that, "In fact, science documents that positive emotions can set off upward spirals in your life, self-sustaining trajectories of growth that lift you up to become a better version of yourself."

In the past, we tried to broaden and build from a faulty foundation where the bedrock was made out of fear, anxiety, and self-doubt. Thinking that perfectionism would help us reach our goals, we never sought a different way—until now.

It is at this moment you step onto solid ground, rooted in the knowing of your strengths, and release the blind spots of your past that were created from faulty thinking. It is from this place of love for yourself and your life that you begin to broaden and build a life of your dreams. Welcome home.

Daily Detox

* Take a self-forgiveness day. One day a week where you refuse, simply refuse, to beat yourself up about anything. On this day, if you do find yourself in a negative conversation with yourself, donate $5 to your favorite charity. That is $5 for each conversation!
* Whenever you start gnawing at yourself, pause, sit, and close your eyes. Take a few deep breaths and now repeat the following to yourself, "May I be safe, May I be peaceful, May I be kind to myself, May I accept myself as I am." I first saw this widely-used

mantra in *Self-Compassion*, a book by Kristin Neff, and have used it since. This loving kindness meditation helps you move into the present and unhook you from the actions, big and small, of your past.

❖ Give yourself a hug. Close your eyes and congratulate yourself. You did it. You took the time to look at the affliction of perfectionism and decided to choose a different way to live. This is huge and don't underrate the hard work and commitment that it took. P.S Self-hugs are not only reserved for this step; they're a recommended lifelong habit.

Never ever forget that the world would rather have your imperfect voice, than your perfect silence.

Notes

xxiv **when it comes to self-reflection:** Pam A. Mueller and Daniel M. Oppenheimer, "The Pen Is Mightier Than the Keyboard," *Psychological Science* 25, no. 6 (2014): 1159–1168, doi:10.1177/0956797614524581.

xxiv **help reduce intrusive thoughts and improve memory:** Siri Carpenter, "A New Reason for Keeping a Diary," *American Psychological Association* 32, no. 8 (September 2001): 68.

8 **creating new habits often revolves around a keystone habit:** Charles Duhigg, *The Power of Habit: Why We Do What We Do and How to Change* (London: Random House Books, 2013).

14 **Experts in the psychology field began calling this "rumination":** Christopher Bergland, "The Brain Mechanics of Rumination and Repetitive Thinking," *Psychology Today*, August 01, 2015, https://www.psychologytoday.com/blog/the-athletes-way/201508/the-brain-mechanics-rumination-and-repetitive-thinking.

14 **repetitive thinking as one of the biggest predicators of depression, anxiety, and stress:** Denise Winterman, "Rumination: The Danger of Dwelling," BBC News, October 17, 2013, http://www.bbc.com/news/magazine-24444431.

15 **self-focused rumination breeds negatively biased thinking:** Sonja Lyubomirsky and Susan Nolen-Hoeksema, "Effects of Self-Focused Rumination on Negative Thinking and Interpersonal Problem Solving," *Journal of Personality and Social Psychology* 69, no. 1 (1995): 176–190. doi:10.1037//0022-3514.69.1.176

15 **solving the problem that caused this feeling in the first place:** Paraphrased from Sonja Lyubomirsky, *The How of Happiness: A New Approach to Getting the Life You Want* (London: Piatkus, 2010), 112.

15 **a little blue or depressed (just like the research says):** Susan Nolen-Hoeksema, Blair E. Wisco, and Sonja Lyubomirsky, "Rethinking Rumination," *Perspectives on Psychological Science* 3, no. 5 (2008): 400–424, doi:10.1111/j.1745-6924.2008.00088.x.

16 **as with any habit rumination can also have triggers:** Edward R. Watkins, "Four Tips from Habit Research to Reduce Worry and Rumination," *Psychology Today*, July 28, 2013, https://www.psychologytoday.com/blog/mood-thought/201307/four-tips-habit-research-reduce-worry-and-rumination.

17 **based upon which thoughts we cling to:** Catherine M. Pittman and Elizabeth M. Karle, *Rewire Your Anxious Brain: How to Use the Neuroscience of Fear to End Anxiety, Panic, and Worry* (Strawberry Hills, NSW: ReadHowYouWant, 2016).

17 **it is important to fill the space with something positive:** Richard M. Wenzlaff and Daniel M. Wegner, "Thought Suppression," *Annual Review of Psychology* 51, no. 1 (2000): 59–91, doi:10.1146/annurev.psych.51.1.59; University of Liverpool, "Dwelling on Negative Events Biggest Cause of Stress," https://news.liverpool.ac.uk/2013/10/17/dwelling-on-negative-events-biggest-cause-of-stress/.

19 **at the end of a long day:** Kelly McGonigal, *The Willpower Instinct: How Self-Control Works, Why It Matters, and What You Can Do to Get More of It* (New York: Avery, 2013).

20 **can have a positive effect on rumination:** B. L. Alderman, R. L. Olson, C. J. Brush, and T. J. Shors, "MAP Training: Combining Meditation and Aerobic Exercise Reduces Depression and Rumination While Enhancing Synchronized Brain Activity," *Translational Psychiatry* 6, no. 2 (2016), doi:10.1038/tp.2015.225.

20 **Pick a positive thought:** M. D. Sacchet et al., "Attention Drives Synchronization of Alpha and Beta Rhythms between Right Inferior Frontal and Primary Sensory Neocortex," *Journal of Neuroscience* 35, no. 5 (2015): 2074–2082, doi:10.1523/jneurosci.1292-14.2015.

23 **expected him to know all the answers:** Sarah Robb O'Hagan and Simon Sinek at Heleo's Cocktails and Conversation. April 21 2017, https://vimeo.com/214180083.

28 **expectations built around perfection:** Centre for Clinical Interventions (CCI), "Perfectionism in Perspective," http://www.cci.health.wa.gov.au/resources/infopax.cfm?Info_ID=52.

36 **making a mistake on the job is their worst fear:** Chad Brooks, "Employees Reveal Their Biggest Work Fears," *Business News Daily*, October 25, 2012, http://www.businessnewsdaily.com/3323-employees-reveal-their-biggest-work-fears.html.

39 **being impeccable with my words:** Don Miguel Ruiz, *The Four Agreements: A Practical Guide to Personal Freedom* (San Rafael, CA: Amber-Allen, 1997).

41 **both exaggerated and beatable:** Pavel G. Somov, *Present Perfect: A Mindfulness Approach to Letting Go of Perfectionism and the Need for Control* (Oakland, CA: New Harbinger, 2010).

46 **knowing that we are worthy of happiness:** Nathaniel Branden, *The Six Pillars of Self-Esteem* (New York: Bantam, 2004).

46 **a small yet profound book:** The tenth anniversary edition is *Have You Filled a Bucket Today?: A Guide to Daily Happiness for Kids*, by Carol McCloud with illustrations by David Messing (Northville, MI: Ferne Press, 2006).

55 **a recognition of our common humanity:** Kristin Neff, *Self-Compassion: Stop Beating Yourself Up and Leave Insecurity Behind* (London: Hodder & Stoughton, 2011).

56 **happiness habits and how often they "practiced" them:** University of Hertfordshire, "Self-Acceptance Could Be the Key to a Happier Life, yet It's the Happy Habit Many People Practice the Least," *ScienceDaily*, March 7, 2014, www.sciencedaily.com/releases/2014/03/140307111016.htm.

57 **a higher level of life satisfaction:** "The Secrets of Happiness," *Psychology Today*, July 1, 1992, https://www.psychologytoday.com/articles/199207/the-secrets-happiness.

62 **stems from our intellect and is focused on our actions:** Gerald Loren Fishkin, *The Science of Shame and Its Treatment* (Marion, MI: Parkhurst Brothers, 2016).

65 **" . . . the self feels wounded from within":** Jane Bolton, "What We Get Wrong about Shame," *Psychology Today*, May 18, 2009, https://www.psychologytoday.com/blog/your-zesty-self/200905/what-we-get-wrong-about-shame.

78 **from a "fixed" to a "growth" mindset:** Carol Dweck, *Mindset: The New Psychology of Success* (New York: Ballantine Books, 2016).

79 **her greatest lessons originated:** Sarah Robb O'Hagan and Greg Lichtenberg, *Extreme You: Step Up. Stand Out. Kick Ass. Repeat.* (New York: HarperBusiness, 2017).

92 **choosing courage over comfort:** Susan A. David, *Emotional Agility: Get Unstuck, Embrace Change, and Thrive in Work and Life* (New York: Avery, 2016), 180–181.

96 **checks their phone more than 157 times per day:** Social Media Week New York, "Millennials Check Their Phones More Than 157 Times per Day." January 18, 2017, https://socialmediaweek.org/newyork/2016/05/31/millennials-check-phones-157-times-per-day/.

96   **"The true scarce commodity will be human attention.":** "You Now Have a Shorter Attention Span Than a Goldfish," *Time*, May 14, 2015, http://time.com/3858309/attention-spans-goldfish/.

97   **the sixty extra days a year:** "How Much Time Do People Spend on Their Mobile Phones in 2017?," *Hacker Noon*, May 9, 2017, https://hackernoon.com/how-much-time-do-people-spend-on-their-mobile-phones-in-2017-e5f90a0b10a6.

97   **sixty thousand times faster:** Rachel Gillett, "Why We're More Likely to Remember Content with Images and Video (Infographic)," *Fast Company*, September 18, 2014, https://www.fastcompany.com/3035856/why-were-more-likely-to-remember-content-with-images-and-video-infogr.

97   **as little as thirteen milliseconds:** Anne Trafton, "In the Blink of an Eye," *MIT News*, January 16, 2014, http://news.mit.edu/2014/in-the-blink-of-an-eye-0116.

98   **the Dove self-esteem project:** "Our Research," Dove US, https://www.dove.com/us/en/stories/about-dove/our-research.html.

101 **(or trying to) go to sleep:** Deloitte, "Global Mobile Consumer Survey: US Edition," https://www2.deloitte.com/us/en/pages/technology-media-and-telecommunications/articles/global-mobile-consumer-survey-us-edition.html.

114 **confessing to being chronic procrastinators:** John Tierney, "Positive Procrastination, Not an Oxymoron," *New York Times*, January 14, 2013, http://www.nytimes.com/2013/01/15/science/positive-procrastination-not-an-oxymoron.html.

115 **serious consequences to our health and happiness:** Sonia Rahimi, Nathan C. Hall, and Timothy A. Pychyl, "Attributions of Responsibility and Blame for Procrastination Behavior," *Frontiers in Psychology* 7 (2016), doi:10.3389/fpsyg.2016.01179.

124 **can make a difference in our results:** Maria Konnikova, "How People Learn to Become Resilient," *New Yorker*, June 19, 2017, http://www.newyorker.com/science/maria-konnikova/the-secret-formula-for-resilience.

125 **we need to think along the lines of:** Rebecca, "Edith Grotberg I Have, I Am, I Can," Aspiral Youth Partners Association, February 6, 2014, http://youthpartners.ca/wordpress/edith-grotberg-i-have-i-am-i-can/.

131 **Being a benefit seeker:** I first heard this terminology during my yearlong study in positive psychology with Tal Ben-Shahar.

131 **with an increase of more than 18 percent between 2005 and 2015:** World Health Organization, "'Depression: Let's Talk' Says WHO, as Depression Tops List of Causes of Ill Health" (press release), http://www.who.int/mediacentre/news/releases/2017/world-health-day/en/.

132 **occurs on a physiological level in the brain:** Susan Reynolds, "Happy Brain, Happy Life," *Psychology Today*, August 2, 2011, https://www.psychologytoday.com/blog/prime-your-gray-cells/201108/happy-brain-happy-life.

133 **more positive moments than negative:** Martin E. P. Seligman, Peter Railton, Roy F. Baumeister, and Chandra Sripada, "Navigating into the Future or Driven by the Past," *Perspectives on Psychological Science* 8, no. 2 (2013): 119–141. doi:10.1177/1745691612474317; Martin E. P. Seligman and John Tierney, "We Aren't Built to Live in the Moment," *New York Times*, May 19, 2017, https://www.nytimes.com /2017/05/19/opinion/sunday/why-the-future-is-always-on-your-mind.html; Avraham N. Kluger and Dina Nir, "The Feedforward Interview," *Human Resource Management Review* 20, no. 3 (2010): 235–246. doi:10.1016/j.hrmr.2009.08.002.

134 **where we choose to place our attention:** Sonja Lyubomirsky, Kennon M. Sheldon, and David Schkade, "Pursuing Happiness: The Architecture of Sustainable Change," *Review of General Psychology* 9, no. 2 (2005): 111–131, doi:10.1037 /1089-2680.9.2.111.

138 **on both our health and happiness:** Ellen J. Langer, *Counterclockwise: Mindful Health and the Power of Possibility* (New York: Ballantine Books, 2009).

138 **boost their happiness in just two weeks:** Yuna L. Ferguson and Kennon M. Sheldon, "Trying to Be Happier Really Can Work: Two Experimental Studies," *Journal of Positive Psychology* 8, no. 1 (2013): 23–33. doi:10.1080/17439760.2012.747000.

142 **through positive interaction and feedback:** Annamarie Mann and Nate Dvorak, "Employee Recognition: Low Cost, High Impact," *Gallup News*, June 28, 2016, http:// news.gallup.com/businessjournal/193238/employee-recognition-low-cost-high-impact .aspx.

142 **these negative things become a part of who you are:** "How the Brain Takes Criticism," *CBS News*, March 2, 2014, https://www.cbsnews.com/news/how-the-brain-takes -criticism/2/.

143 **this becomes your mistake, not theirs:** Roger Marek, Cornelia Strobel, Timothy W. Bredy, and Pankaj Sah, "The Amygdala and Medial Prefrontal Cortex: Partners in the Fear Circuit," *Journal of Physiology* 591, no. 10 (2013): 2381–2391, doi:10.1113 /jphysiol.2012.248575.

151 **being diligent, productive, and effective:** Bahtiyar Eraslan Çapan, "Relationship among Perfectionism, Academic Procrastination and Life Satisfaction of University Students," *Procedia—Social and Behavioral Sciences* 5 (2010): 1665–1671, doi:10.1016/j.sbspro.2010.07.342; Sherrie Campbell, "A Rigid Mind Blocks Success: Try These 5 Strategies for Fearless Leadership," *Entrepreneur*, November 20, 2014, https://www.entrepreneur.com/article/239892; Áine Cain, "11 Signs Your Boss Is a Perfectionist," *Business Insider*, September 16, 2016, http://www.businessinsider.com /signs-your-boss-is-a-perfectionist-2016-9.

156 **still feel the behavior is undesirable:** Ellen J. Langer, *Mindfulness* (Boston: Da Capo Press, 2014).

161 **triggers the same part of our brains as many antidepressants:** Patrick J. Smith and James A. Blumenthal, "Exercise and Physical Activity in the Prevention and Treatment of Depression," *Routledge Handbook of Physical Activity and Mental Health*, doi:10.4324/9780203132678.ch8; "Study: Exercise Has Long-Lasting Effect on Depression," *Duke Today*, https://today.duke.edu/2000/09/exercise922.html.

170 **our world will expand as the result:** Todd Kashdan, "The Power of Curiosity," *Experience Life*, May 1, 2010, https://experiencelife.com/article/the-power-of-curiosity/.

171 **it also improves information retention:** Matthias J. Gruber, Bernard D. Gelman, and Charan Ranganath, "States of Curiosity Modulate Hippocampus-Dependent Learning via the Dopaminergic Circuit," *Neuron* 84, no. 2 (2014): 486–496, doi:10.1016/j.neuron.2014.08.060.

172 **that would otherwise go unnoticed:** Bernadette Jiwa, *Hunch: Turn Your Everyday Insights into the Next Big Thing* (New York: Portfolio/Penguin, 2017).

175 **good for our mind and great for our happiness:** Emily Campbell, "Six Surprising Benefits of Curiosity," *Greater Good Magazine*, https://greatergood.berkeley.edu/article/item/six_surprising_benefits_of_curiosity.

175 **comes with the rigid thinking of perfectionism:** Fredrik Saboonchi and Lars-Gunnar Lundh, "Perfectionism, Self-Consciousness and Anxiety," *Personality and Individual Differences* 22, no. 6 (1997): 921–928, doi:10.1016/s0191-8869(96)00274-7.

175 **the lowered risk of anxiety disorders:** Curiosity may also be relevant to the development of psychopathology because an intolerance of uncertainty has been demonstrated to be an important risk factor for anxiety disorders (Dugas, Freeston, & Ladouceur, 1997). James F. Boswell, Johanna Thompson-Hollands, Todd J. Farchione, and David H. Barlow, "Intolerance of Uncertainty: A Common Factor in the Treatment of Emotional Disorders," *Journal of Clinical Psychology* 69, no. 6 (2013): 630–645, doi:10.1002/jclp.21965.

175 **up and out of the more challenging times:** Research on the benefits of curiosity is only beginning to accumulate. Among other adaptive outcomes, curiosity is suspected to play a role in the development of intelligence, wisdom, happiness, meaning in life, distress tolerance, and satisfying and engaging social relationships (for reviews, see Kashdan, 2009; Renninger, Hidi, & Krapp, 1992; Silvia, 2006) Todd B. Kashdan, Paul Rose, and Frank D. Fincham, "Curiosity and Exploration: Facilitating Positive Subjective Experiences and Personal Growth Opportunities," *Journal of Personality Assessment* 82, no. 3 (2004): 291–305, doi:10.1207/s15327752jpa8203_05.

181 **" . . . while cutting learning times in half":** Vala Afshar, "Training Your Mind to Achieve Ultimate Performance," *Huffington Post*, March 26, 2017, https://www.huffingtonpost.com/entry/training-your-mind-to-achieve-ultimate-performance_us_58d82bb2e4b0c0980ac0e751.

182 **they just played without pressure:** Charles J. Limb and Allen R. Braun, "Neural Substrates of Spontaneous Musical Performance: An fMRI Study of Jazz Improvisation," *PLOS ONE* 3, no. 2 (2008), doi:10.1371/journal.pone.0001679.

183 **has eight components:** Mihaly Csikszentmihalyi, *Flow: The Psychology of Optimal Experience* (New York: HarperPerennial ModernClassics, 2008).

183 **created a flow condition checklist:** Owen Schaffer, "Crafting Fun User Experiences—A Method to Facilitate Flow," Human Factors International, http://human factors.com/whitepapers/crafting_fun_ux.asp.

195 **" . . . no matter their circumstances":** Barbara Fredrickson, *Love 2.0: How Our Supreme Emotion Affects Everything We Think, Do, Feel, and Become* (New York: Hudson Street Press, 2013).

203 **their ideal future and best future selves:** Laura A. King, "The Health Benefits of Writing about Life Goals," *Personality and Social Psychology Bulletin* 27, no. 7 (2001): 798–807, doi:10.1177/0146167201277003.

205 **" . . . to become a better version of yourself":** Barbara Frederickson, *Love 2.0: How Our Supreme Emotion Affects Everything We Think, Do, Feel, and Become* (New York: Hudson Street Press, 2013).

Acknowledgments

"Feeling gratitude and not expressing it is like wrapping a present and not giving it."

—WILLIAM ARTHUR WARD

N FULL DISCLOSURE, I TOTALLY PROCRASTINATED ON THIS SECTION UNTIL THE FINAL HOUR. THE thought of not writing the perfect acknowledgments page, or the idea of leaving out anyone who was important to the evolution of this book, was overwhelming to say the least. (I am deeply sorry if I missed you. I promise I will make it up to you with a hug and a glass of your favorite wine!)

This book would never have reached your hands if it were not for my literary agent Stephen Hanselman and his amazing wife Julia Serebrinsky. Writing a book is one thing and writing a book proposal is another. Thank you for your friendship, guidance and continued support during the entire process. You are two of my biggest champions and I am eternally grateful to you both.

Gretchen Lees, my sage and writing mentor. I could not have gotten this book across the finish line without you. Your expert eyes, your precision edits and your ability to keep me going when I thought I did not have another creative word inside of me is a special gift. Thank you for sharing your extraordinary talents, your expertise and your fantastic one-liners (darn you are good) with me and within this book.

To everyone at Da Capo Lifelong: you made this process such an enjoyable journey. Renée Sedliar, thank you for believing in this material and for creating such a collaborative experience. Cisca Schreefel and Martha Whitt, thank you for your eagle eyes and perfect edits, and Miriam Riad, thank you for keeping everything organized. Anna Dorfman, my heart exploded when I saw the book cover you created; thank you for your inspired and beautiful design which perfectly captured the message inside.

To my dearest Jennie: you are my sister, my best friend, my confidant and my travel buddy. I love you so much. You are my family. We are small but mighty. Thank you for being such a source of goodness in my life.

To my cherished friends who supported and loved me long before this book was even in my imagination. You have always celebrated with me during my highlight moments and you have kept my heart beating during the more difficult times. Thank you for always being there for me. No matter what time it is or where in the world I may be, I know you will pick up the phone: Molly Fox, Jon Giswold, Denise Klatte, Brandon Neff, Betsy Parker, Howard Schissler, Jeffrey Scott, Melanie Smith and Lisa Wheeler, I will never take our friendship for granted. I hope you know how much I love you.

To my dear friends and book mentors Jenny Blake and Dorie Clark. I could not have wished for two more generous souls to come into my life at the perfect time. Thank you for your endless wisdom, advice and celebration dinners.

To Michael Pipitone and Mike Babbitt, thank you for bringing such a rocking soundtrack to my life and for your love and support on my DJ adventures.

To Jonathan and Stephanie Fields, it was during The Art of Becoming Known that this book was born. Thank you for all of your support and for allowing me to share my message through your many platforms.

Jay Blahnik, I will never forget the guidance you offered to me on that rainy day, during your cab ride back to Newark Airport. Thank you for encouraging me to step into the white powder of the still to be written future. Now here it is in print.

Patricia Moreno, thank you for hosting the first ever Perfection Detox workshop; it planted a seed that became my purpose and passion. To Caroline Kohles at the Marlene Meyerson JCC, and to Angela Leigh at Pure Yoga West NYC, thank you for allowing me to use your beautiful spaces to teach, tweak and fine-tune my material.

Tal Ben-Shahar, Maria Sirois, Megan McDonough and all the participants in year two of the Certificate In Positive Psychology, I thank you. My year with you changed the work of my past into my calling for the future.

Sara Allen, thank you for keeping my work and calling organized and on time.

To the beautiful and brave women who shared their stories and struggles with me: Anne, Jennifer, Joanna, Julie, Laurie, Lindsay, Lisa, Lucy, Rocky and Terry, your voices have helped us all feel a little less alone on this journey.

I am so deeply grateful to the beautiful women who went through the online version of this program. Your input helped me get super clear around my message. Amy, Barb, Cheryl, Christine, Connie, Corina, Deb, Denise, Diane, Gay, Grace, Heidi, Hilari, Jan, Jane, Jennifer, Jillian, Lucy, Mary, Maria, Molly, Michelle, Nancy, Rocky, Sarah and Tammy, thank you for sharing your hearts and experiences with me.

There are so many who have helped me stand where I am today: Tim Amos, Mindy Bacharach, Jamie Broderick, Tricia Brouk, Rick Clemmons, Scott Cole, Sarah Collins, Lashaun Dale, Lisa Delaney, Shannon Fable, Jen Groover, Jeri Speicher Gutner, Julie Hunt, Carol Ientile, Rich Kieling, Matthew Kimberley, Constance Klein, Susie Moore, Iris Schenk, Luba Winegardner, and Christian Zamora I am so grateful to know you.

To my fitness mentors, if we have been on a brochure or a schedule together, or passed in the hallways at a conference, please know that you have been a source of inspiration to me. You made me step up, work hard and continually challenge myself as a presenter, and for that I thank you.

A special fitness thank you to: Alice Bracegirdle, Shannon Elkins, Kimberly Spreen-Glick, Rob Glick, Maureen Hagan, Sara Kooperman, Jamie Nicholls, and Mike Spezzano. You were the first to give me an opportunity to step out of my sneakers and into real clothes as a presenter. I am so grateful for your trust and encouragement as I transitioned into writing and speaking. My hips, back and knees also thank you.

To my fitness family who has been working out with me for over thirty years, I have cherished sweating through the decades with you. It is impossible to name all of you here, but to anyone that has ever done a grapevine, taken a step class or completed a Mambo Cha Cha with me, thank you for sharing your hearts, your energy, your support and your smiles.

I cannot go without mentioning The Writers Room in New York City. You gave me a quiet space where I could hear my thoughts and bring them to life. I do not know how I would have finished this book on time without your sanctuary. It was also extremely helpful to realize I was not the only writer who sometimes struggled to find that perfect next word.

Last but certainly not least, thank you dear reader for sharing your heart and your time with me. I hope that this is just the beginning of a flourishing friendship between us. I am looking forward to staying connected and hearing about all of the wonderful things that unfold for you.

One last thing before I go. Right now (unless it's super late) I invite you to send a quick gratitude text to someone who makes your day a little brighter. If I had your phone number, you would be receiving one from me and it would read:

> *I truly am grateful for the time we shared together.*
> *May you never again forget how special you are.*
> *Welcome home.*

Index

About
the Author

PETRA KOLBER IS AN INTERNATIONALLY RENOWNED FITNESS EXPERT AND WELLNESS LEADER who is known throughout the industry as a crusader for change and a beacon of authentic happiness. In her twenty-five years in the fitness world she has starred in and choreographed sixty award-winning videos and fitness programs, and has spoken live to thousands of motivated followers. As a national workshop leader and keynote speaker she inspires people around the globe to stand up for their lives and live profoundly from their hearts. She has been a consultant and contributor to many national fitness magazines and has been named Fitness Crusader of the Year by *Health* magazine. She has been the face and voice of leading food and fitness companies such as Reebok, Spry Living, Yes Fitness Music, and California Walnuts.

As a two-time cancer survivor, she is passionate about waking people up to the precious gift of time. Her mission is to inspire people to move more and fear less, so that they can stretch their dreams, strengthen their courage muscle and build an inspired life, full of joy and gratitude.

In her spare time Petra is an aspiring DJ, a budding cook, an avid traveler, and podcast maven who feels deeply blessed on the mornings she can wake up early enough to watch the sunrise.